The Let.

Variant Readings of Genesis 3/:3 in the Andəmta
Corpus

The Letter That Kills

Variant Readings of Genesis 37:3

in the *Andəmta* Corpus

Alem Sahle

AGORA
UNIVERSITY
PRESS
EST. 2012

The Letter That Kills: Variant Readings of Genesis 37:3 in the Andəmta Corpus

For more information, contact: aupress@agora.edu
Agora University Press: press.agora.ac
ISBN 978-1-950831-45-6 (print)
      978-1-950831-46-3 (ebook)
Printed in the United States of America

HIS HOLINESS POPE TAWADROS II
118th Pope and Patriarch of the great city of Alexandria and the See of St. Mark.

HIS HOLINESS PATRIARCH IGNATIUS APHREM II
Patriarch of Antioch and All the East.

Table of Contents

Introduction

Hidden in the rugged highlands of Ethiopia is a nearly two-thousand-year-old expression of an indigenous Afro-Semitic Christianity, the Ethiopian Orthodox *Täwahədo*[1] Church. Surrounded by Islam on all sides, the medieval Christian kingdom of Ethiopia and its *Täwahədo* faith were effectively cut off from the rest of the known world for more than 1200 years. Despite this, it is known for preserving a strikingly vivid manifestation of biblical Christianity, a stark Afro-Asiatic spirituality that one might imagine when reading the Scriptures. This reality is immediately evident upon first glance at its original indigenous religious expressions, such as its magnificent liturgical and iconographic traditions, but survival has not been its main achievement; rather, in secret,

---

[1] *Täwahədo* (ተዋሕዶ) is the Ethiopic term expressing "oneness," referring to the notion of μια φυσις in Cyril of Alexandria's formula and is a declaration of One Incarnate Nature—from two natures. This is often denoted the pejorative *Monophysite* but is instead a *Miaphysite* Christology, which is the teaching of all Oriental Orthodox Churches. This Christology was called into question and debated by Ethiopians in the 16th and 17th centuries amid local controversies and debates both internally and with European missionaries. The divisions were among the Unction ቅባት and the Grace ጸጋ (or Three Births ሦስት ልደት) sects. It has become customary since then to refer to the church not only as the Ethiopian Orthodox but additionally, as the *Täwahədo* Church. See Mebratu Kiros Gebru, *Miaphysite Christology: An Ethiopian Perspective* (Piscataway: Gorgias Press, 2009), 19-72. For a Ge'ez critical edition of a document professing the Unction Christology see Getatchew Haile, ed., *The Faith of The Unctionists In The Ethiopian Church (Haymanot Mäsihawit)*, vol. 517 of *Corpus Scriptorum Christianorum Orientalium* (Louvain: Peeters Publishers, n.d.).119

the faith thrived producing a body of knowledge within its traditional schools, one of which is the school of Biblical commentary (*Andəmta Tərgʷame Bet*). Until very recently in the 21st century, the *Andəmta* tradition remained unknown even to the majority of Ethiopian society—minus those who pass through the Ethiopian ecclesiastical education system—let alone to Western academics. The British Orientalist, Roger W. Cowley (d. 1988), who initiated the beginnings of western recognition and scholarship of this field remarked that "it is as if one had suddenly discovered the entire Talmud!" The *Andəmta* masters (*mämhərän*) were immersed in a life of scholarship at the highest stage of education in the Ethiopian Orthodox Täwahədo Church. They were often found with their disciples tucked away in monastic communities, clandestine settings such as church graveyards, or at times even in the simple home of their teacher. Here students would gather, one would read a verse in a solemn tone (*wərd nəbāb*), and the master would proceed to exegete the verse, elucidating it with a piece of commentary, then saying "*andəm*," "there is also another […]," to introduce additional commentary. These lessons would be committed to memory, and this procedure would continue until the student had memorized not only the entire text but also the commentary by heart. Through years of such pedagogy, the student would complete his studies and become a teacher in his field of commentary.

There are four fields taught in the traditional Ethiopian biblical commentary schools: New Testament (*Ḥaddis Kidān*), Old Testament (*Bəluy Kidān)*, Patristic Books (*Mäṣḥāfä Liqāwnt*), and Monastic Books (*Mäṣḥāfä*

Mänäkosat). Some of the more notable masters would not only pass on what they had learned *verbatim* but would also venture to find new interpretations to the Biblical text.[2]

They would do this by examining all texts at their disposal and striving to attain more sources; in this way, they would incorporate a great wealth of knowledge into the tradition. These sources would be drawn from Arabic, Syriac, Hebrew, and Greek languages, emanating heavily from authors of Syriac and other Oriental Christian dispensations. Some of these texts would be directly translated; others would be used as inspiration for the Ethiopian scholar's own creative work. Professor Getatchew Haile, the world's premier Ge'ez philologist observed that the Ethiopian literary tradition "contains both original works and translations from foreign sources."[3] He describes the geographical setting in medieval times as "a country surrounded by nations with little or no literary traditions."[4] He remarks, "our ancestors, therefore, received little inspiration from their neighbors,"[5] and described the perilous journey to the Christian Orient that lay before those who wished to find literary inspiration as one which resulted in many Ethiopians perishing at the hands of highwaymen

---

[2] Prime examples of masters who strived to improve upon the body of knowledge are *Mämahir Esdros*, and *Mämahir Kaflä Giyorgis*, these details are elaborated in Chapter 3.

[3] Getatchew Haile, "Highlighting Traditional Ethiopian Literature," in *Silence Is Not Golden: A Critical Anthology of Ethiopian Literature* (Lawrenceville: Red Sea Press, 1995), 39.

[4] Ibid.

[5] Ibid.

and religious enemies, falling prey to wild animals and succumbing to the stings of scorpions and other poisonous insects in search of inspiring ideas.[6] In this way, they would trek to Egypt, Cyprus, the Holy Land, and at times even travel as far as Armenia to return home with books which they would then translate into Ge'ez.[7] These books were not limited to commentary on Scripture but also manuscripts of the text of Scripture itself.

It is scandalous for some to learn that these scholars were not only trying to attain a better understanding of Scripture (through commentary) but also a more accurate reading of it. Said another way, some of the most outstanding Ethiopian scholars believed that the Ge'ez Scriptures were imperfect, and they labored to revise these very texts themselves! One of the most prominent *Andəmta* masters to ever live—circa the 18th century—*Mämhər Esdros* is even said to have articulated without fear, that the text is *defective*. He is known to have dedicated the latter years of his life to editing the text by critiquing it against more authoritative manuscripts[8]—*an approach to literary scholarship hereafter referred to simply as textual criticism.* This view was not limited to just the celebrated teachers; rather, it will be shown in this research that it is an axiom implicit within the tradition itself. The evidenced for this will be established by its style of exegesis;[9] which gives light to the core

---

[6] Ibid.

[7] Ibid.

[8] See Mersha Alehegne, *The Ethiopian Commentary on the Book of Genesis*, (Wiesbaden: Otto Harrassowitz, 2011), 10.

[9] Ibid.

hermeneutical philosophy that is at play within the corpus of
the Ethiopian commentary literature. This hermeneutic will
be define, examined, and studied in its literary depth.

It will be argued that the core hermeneutic
philosophy of the Ethiopian tradition can be defined and
summarized by a common adage within the *Andəmta*
commentary tradition, "the letter kills, but the interpretation
gives life" (**ንባብ፡ይቀትል፡ወትርጓሜ፡ያሐዩ፡**). This phrase is
usually uttered whenever there is challenging wording,
variant readings, or a defect within the manuscript. It is
rooted in 2 Corinthians 3: 6, "the letter kills but the spirit
gives life" and can be found in the Pauline *Andəmta*
commentary section of that verse.[10] The greatest of the
Ethiopian scholars were not alone in this opinion; we see
them in agreement here with the Christianity of antiquity and
we see that the adage mentioned has always been the
fundamental hermeneutic philosophy of the Church since its
birth in the 1st century CE.

The text-critical approach of the Ethiopian Biblical
commentary tradition contrasts with the view of textual
completeness commonly held within the church. This view
of textual completeness, which raises the text above
correction, results in a poor state of Biblical scholarship.
Additionally, this perspective requires one to turn a blind eye
to the long history of Biblical studies native to the land. This

---

[10] *YäQəddus Pawulos Mäṣhäf Nəbab KänäTərgʷame*—የቅዱስ ጳውሎስ
መጽሐፍ ንባቡ ከነትርጓሜው [*The Pauline Writings with Commentary*]
(Addis Ababa, 1946), 207.

research will refute the view of textual completeness by showing that the text-critical perspective is aligned with the Biblical scholarship of the early Church. It will be seen then that the *Andəmta* commentary tradition, at its core, lives in continuation of this, as a tradition that interprets the Scriptures not with a fixation on the letter, but with a focus on the spirit of the text.

The specific scope of this research will concentrate on text-critical examples where the letter of the Scriptural text is critiqued and corrected by Ethiopian scholars, a somewhat common occurrence in the *Andəmta*. These examples will be the literary data upon which the previously mentioned adage is established as a core hermeneutic philosophy.

The methodology by which this will be achieved is as follows:

I. The hermeneutic question regarding the correct interpretation of a reading that has difficult textual qualities or variants will be answered in Chapter 2 by first looking at variations in the text of the Old Testament used by early Christians and Second Temple Jewish communities. This will lead to the discussion of the efficacy of the Scriptural text in conveying Divine revelation, and ultimately the relationship between the text and its spirit (or, its *correct* understanding). This will be viewed from the perspective of exegetes of the early Church, particularly Origen, St. Ephrem the Syrian, and St. Gregory of Nazianzus who all clearly convey the superiority of the spirit over the text's linguistic qualities. This will allow us to summarize the capacity of the Scriptures in conveying revelation of the Divine Person—i.e., the textual epistemology of Scripture. The focal point of this section will be an examination of Origen's monumental work, the Hexapla, through which variant readings were preserved and propagated throughout the ancient Church, and of particular interest here, the Ethiopian Church.

II. By applying the insights from the previous section to Chapter 3, it will be possible to establish the medieval Ethiopian *Andəmta* commentary tradition as in continuation of the early Church's exegetical legacy. This will be accomplished by exploring the Ethiopian Church's history and lore with regards to the Ge'ez texts of Scripture. This will culminate in a conclusion clearly defining the Ethiopian textual epistemology. In doing so we will also see the difference between the text-critical approach and the view of textual completeness, both of which are found in the Ethiopian Church. Finally, the focal point of this section will be a study of the Ethiopian Church's monumental work of Biblical scholarship, the *Andəmta* corpus. Manuscript evidence will be used to form conclusions about the types of variant readings preserved by this tradition. This data will firmly establish its core hermeneutic philosophy as text-critical and textually transcendent.[11] This core interpretive philosophy will be proven to be summarized in the adage: "the letter kills, but the interpretation gives life" (ነባብ፡ይቀትል፡ወትርጓሜ፡ያሐዩ፡፡), a truly Ethiopian hermeneutic.

These methodological conclusions will open the door for a study of a medieval Ethiopian commentary manuscript in Chapter 4.[12] The manuscript contains evidence pointing to a text-critical edit correcting Scripture via a typological interpretation. The manuscript in particular is a commentary on the Pentateuch compiled by a 16th-century cleric named Məhərka Dəngəl. This manuscript contains two elements that make it a key data point for testing the validity of the conclusions made thus far. These elements are one, evidence of textual diversity with Scripture (i.e. variant readings) one of which is collected from Origen's Hexapla—and two, a subsequent interpretation to align it with the spirit of the text. The interpretation of the text examined in this section is also of particular importance due to the insight it gives into the medieval Ethiopian scholar's mind. The manuscript's internal data tells us a story of how far the *Andəmta* scholars would look for literary inspiration and where in the

---

[11] This categorically rules out the validity of textual completeness, a perspective that requires a total denial of history, manuscript data, and sound theology.

[12] The manuscript found in EMML (Ethiopian Manuscript Microfilm Library) 2101 would have been a source for commentary and represents the type of literary inspiration the tradition was built upon.

broader narrative of Ethiopian history our author, Məhərka Dəngəl fit. This point is of great interest given that the corpus is essentially silent of any biographical information regarding the scholars who forged it. The passage examined here is that of the commentary on Genesis 37:3, concerning the coat which Jacob made for his son Joseph. This pericope will also be studied for the insight it provides regarding the theological theme of suffering.

All of this in summary is aimed at providing historical, biographical, theological, and thematic insight from the Ethiopian *Andəmta* tradition.

Chapter 1

Literature Review

Introduction

Western scholarship of the Ethiopian Biblical commentary tradition did not begin until about 1970 CE. The reasons for this are the same as why it evaded Ethiopian society for so long: its linguistic and literary qualities.

From a linguistic perspective, the *Andəmta* tradition requires a mastery of Amharic[13] and Ge'ez.[14] The text of Scripture and additional supporting quotations are in Ge'ez with commentary in Amharic. The Amharic is in a classical form and can vary greatly in its grammar, syntax, and vocabulary from its modern counterpart, making it incomprehensible even to fluent speakers of today.[15] Secondly, it has a broad literary span. The quotations made

---

[13] The national language of Ethiopia.

[14] Also known as "Ethiopic," the ecclesiastical language of the *Täwahədo* churches of Ethiopia and Eritrea.

[15] Cowley references some 21 examples, such as archaic spellings (e.g. አይደለሞና as አይደለትም or አይደለሞናት or አይዶለሞና), the archaic multiplier እለ instead of the modern እነ, use of compound imperfect as relative (መንግስተ፡ሰማይ፡ይፈትሂል፡ሌላን፡አለ።), etc. See Roger W. Cowley, *The Traditional Interpretation of the Apocalypse of St John in the Ethiopian Orthodox Church*, (Cambridge: Cambridge University Press, 2014), 25-26.

within the commentary can range anywhere from the text of Scripture to patristic, liturgical, hagiographical, monastic, and historical writings, personal interpretations of notable masters, or even linguistic arguments referencing Hebrew, Syriac, etc. Additionally, since it is an oral tradition and given its place at the highest stage of the Ethiopian Church's education system, quotations never include text and chapters.[16] Professor Getatchew Haile expresses all the above points as follows:

> To prove the validity of their views, it was the custom for the authors of biblical commentaries to draw upon an extremely wide variety of sources. They cited a wide range of written material, orally transmitted custom, and also used the various meanings of words in different languages. The books they quote include some whose existence in Ge'ez we are not aware of. But the study of commentary material is difficult because the Amharic in which it is preserved is itself very difficult and the identification of quotations from named and unnamed sources requires a full command of the Ge'ez literature from published and unpublished sources scattered

---

[16] This may be due in part to the assumption that the student lives a life of immersion in the church's literary tradition, and is able to locate quotes with relative ease.

all over the world and all over Ethiopian monasteries.[17]

These are the challenges and their related intricacies, which the Cambridge Orientalist Roger Cowley took up and sorted out as he marked the beginning of the modern academic scholarship in the field. Several of his works laid the foundation for examining the hermeneutics of the corpus, its sources, and attempts at identifying authors. Since this research is concerned with these points, and with building further upon them, the review of literature rightly begins here.

Review

In 1963 CE Roger W. Cowley (d. 1988) arrived in Ethiopia from Britain with the Anglican Church's mission to the Ethiopian Jews.[18] His first few journal publications later that decade were solely of an Amharic linguistic concern, *The Standardisation of Amharic Spelling* (1967) and *A and B Verbal Stem-Type in Amharic* (1969) but were not entirely unrelated with regards to commentary. The points established here would resurface in his subsequent works which were more directly related to the *Andəmta* itself.

Preliminary Notes on the Baläandəm Commentaries (1971) was the first of these, it is a general introduction to

---

[17] Getatchew Haile, *Review of The Traditional Interpretation of the Apocalyse of St John in the Ethiopian Orthodox Church (University of Cambridge Oriental Publications, No. 33)*, by Roger W. Cowley, *Rassegna Di Studi Etiopici* 30 (1984), 188.

[18] V. Nersessian, "Roger Cowley (1940-1988)," *Journal of Ethiopian Studies* 22 (1989), 171.

the commentaries. It begins with a description of the four fields of commentary (Old Testament, New Testament, Books of the Monks, and Patristics) in addition to describing the general features of the corpus. He details the contents of the introductory sections of the *Andəmta*, which provide context on the writer and the reason for the work. He then describes the body of the commentary itself and the pattern it follows; he also introduces a few of the many technical terms found within commentary texts.

The Beginnings of the Andəm Commentary Tradition (1972) presents his theory that marginal manuscript[19] annotations were the basis of the development of the commentary tradition: this is a helpful article for those studying Ge'ez manuscript marginalia. It is a comparative study of three manuscripts and contains an examination of the commentary of 1 Samuel 1-31.

Old Testament Introduction in the Andəmta Commentary Tradition (1974) examines the introductory sections of the Old Testament commentary in detail. It discusses the elaborations on the writer's name, meaning and significance, matters relating to the book and historical background, doctrinal points revealed within the text, and the book's canonicity. Additionally, Cowley provides in the appendix an English translation from Amharic of a chapter titled "The Interpretation of Books" from 'The Ancient

---

[19] Ethiopian manuscripts are often in codex format with the pages consisting of animal skins.

Teaching of Ethiopia' by *Liqä Səltanat Habtä Mariam,*[20] which contains the traditional account of how the *Andəmta* developed. This section includes a rather long and useful list of the notable *mämhərän* and their successors. It is an essential resource for beginning any biographical study of the notable teachers. Identifying any characters is difficult since the corpus is almost entirely silent regarding individuals, and any information is valuable. *New Testament Introduction in the Andəmta Commentary Tradition* (1977) is the New Testament analog to the previous study, and continued interest in the linguistic aspect of the corpus is observed in these articles in addition to the purely linguistic concern in *Additional sources for the Copula TT in Old Amharic* (1977).

Mämhər Esdros and his Interpretations (1980) began a new trajectory for Cowley in which he began studying biographical information. Here, he hypothesizes that the reason for the diffusion of learning and change in textual traditions in the 18th century was due to gifted masters (*mämhərän*). The paper is a study of *Mämhər Esdros* and some of his sample commentaries drawing from Ethiopian historical sources, material culture, oral traditions, and the scarce information about him found within the commentaries themselves. Also, in this study is an appendix of nearly 20 pages with the names of additional scholars and

---

[20] This is Archbishop *Mälkäṣädeq* (Melchizedek). *Liqä Səlṭanat* was his title at the time due to his position as the administrator of Holy Trinity Cathedral in Addis Ababa, he was elevated to the episcopacy under Patriarch Abuna *Märəqorios* (d. 2020).

highlights of some other gifted persons that may be of interest.

A Ge'ez Prologue Concerning the Work of Kəflä Giyorgis (1983) is a second study with a biographical aim. Here he discusses how biographical information on scholars is fragmentary and uses the case of a more recent scholar *Kəflä Giyorgis* (1825-1908 CE) as a basis to gain insight into the life and motives of the Ethiopian scholars. The historical manuscript that is the basis for this study is found in the Ethiopian Church on Ethiopia Street in Jerusalem. This manuscript contains the story of how the commentary on the book of Ezekiel was lost in those times and the lengths to which *Kəflä Giyorgis* went to attain it.

The Blood of Zechariah (Matthew 23:35) in Ethiopian Exegetical Tradition (1983) is the first pericope study on the corpus and is focused on the commentary of Matthew 23:35. The commentary here is concerned with the questions of Zechariah and Barachiah's identity, the murder of Zechariah, the reason for its occurrence near the Temple, and the nature of its parallel with Abel—i.e., the bubbling of the blood. Cowley is also here concerned with the source material and identifies several Jewish and Christian influences. He draws the following conclusions: the exegetical tradition is in continuity with Antiochene and Nestorian exegesis; at times it is difficult to draw trajectories for borrowed sources; the commentary tradition is concerned with questions relevant to moral applications when interpreting a text and not mere curiosity. Cowley also tentatively concludes that the final crystallization of the current corpus and its provenance are (16th – 18th C.E.) Gondar.

Cowley's first book was originally submitted in partial fulfillment of the degree of B.D. at Cambridge University, "The Traditional Interpretation of the Apocalypse of St. John in the Ethiopian Orthodox Church" (1983) is an immense contribution to the study of the corpus. Cowley states that he chose the Apocalypse of St John because it possesses three qualities that no other *Andəmta* section had at the time; a printed edition of the commentary, a critical edition of the Ge'ez text of the Apocalypse of St. John, and it being the most extensively commented upon portion of Scripture in the Ethiopian tradition. Cowley's book is split into three sections, the first describes the corpus, its character, provenance, and development and includes extensive details regarding its linguistic character, historical references, studies on source material, the method by which it is taught, etc. The second part is an annotated translation of the Ge'ez *Tərg^wame Qälämsis* (*Commentary on the Apocalypse*) using the B.L. (British Library) MS Orient 13830. The third part is an annotated translation of the printed Amharic commentary on the Apocalypse together with the text of Scripture in Ge'ez which was printed in 1958 in Addis Ababa under the title *The 3 New Testament Books, Text and Commentary* (*Mäṣḥāftä Ḥaddisat Śostu, Nəbab Känätərg^wame*) by *Liqä Liqawənt Mähari Tərfe*. Cowley draws some comparisons between the manuscript of *Tərg^wame Qälämsis* and the printed edition and it is evident that they differ completely on certain points and even oppose certain views adhered to in Ethiopia. Cowley concludes that the author of the manuscript has drawn on the same material as the commentary learned and taught by *Liqä Liqawənt Mähari Tərfe* but has exercised a more selective and critical judgment. Cowley also suggests that the named sources for the MS are a tradition in an oral or semi-literal form that was known also to the *Andəmta* compilers.

A Ge'ez Document Reporting Controversy Concerning the Bible Commentaries of Ibn at-Taiyib (1987) is a study of a manuscript from EMML (Ethiopian Manuscript Microfilm Library) 7122 f. 51a-b. Cowley provides a copy of this short letter along with an English translation and a study of its provenance, genre, language, author and addressee, historical context, and the doctrinal topics contained within it. The letter is a unique historical example of the controversies that occurred among the Ethiopian Biblical commentary scholars regarding the interpretation of Scriptures. Although controversies are well documented regarding Christology[21] and the Sabbath,[22] this study is unique, and a similar occurrence of manuscript evidence has not yet been discovered.

Cowley's last contribution is a book that was originally submitted for a Doctor of Divinity degree at Cambridge University titled "Ethiopian Biblical

---

[21] See footnote 1.

[22] For a general history of controversies on the Sabbath during the medieval period see Taddesse Tamrat, *Church and State in Ethiopia, 1270-1527* (Oxford: Clarendon Press, 1972), 404. Concerning manuscript evidence from the same period, see Getatchew Haile, "The Letter of Archbishops Mika'el and Gäbrə'el Concerning the Observance of Saturday," *Journal of Semitic Studies* 26.1 (1981): 73–78.

Interpretation: A Study in exegetical tradition and hermeneutics" (1987) and was instigated by a letter from Professor E. Ullendorff stating that "the time has surely come now to assess in some detail both provenance and the nature of the Ethiopian hermeneutical material."[23] The work aims to answer the question "with which exegetical tradition(s) does the traditional Biblical (and Patristic) Amharic commentary material of the Ethiopian Orthodox Church stand in essential continuity, and what are the processes that have made this tradition what it is?"

The book consists of six parts, the first is the introduction, and the second is titled "Methodological Soundings" where Cowley begins with eight pericope studies of the commentary material: the chronology of Noah's flood (Genesis 7-8), a tradition concerning the number of the written and unwritten languages of the descendants of Noah (Genesis 11:7-9), the ancestry of Melchizedek (Genesis 14), the *Diamerismos tes ges* (Joshua 6-7), "One who came from Edom" (Isaiah 63:1), Simeon (Luke 2:25), the magi (Matthew 2), and finally the sinful woman who anointed Jesus (Matthew 26).

Comparisons are drawn here between the *Andəmta*, Jewish, Oriental Christian—Arabic, Syriac, Coptic—and Greek commentaries. Cowley has studied the relevant works of the peripheral traditions but was "careful not to be influenced by their conclusions or base his study on

---

[23] Cowley *op. cit.*, vii.

theirs."[24] It is satisfying how thoroughly acquainted he was here with the Ethiopian sources themselves and those years he spent living with the *Andəmta* scholars in Gondar are evident.[25] As for the reason why these short studies were used as a methodological basis, he explains this through a quote by P. Tillich that "every methodological reflection is abstracted from the cognitive work in which one engages [...] it never precedes it,"[26] i.e., it is the motifs that Cowley previously studied, which lead him to his examinations of methodology. The "question of the direct use of Jewish sources in Ethiopian commentaries" is followed by the main body of the work which consists of Chapters 4 and 5. Chapter 4 examines the theme of creation and consists of the Ge'ez text—using Dillmann's critical edition of the Octateuch[27]—and an annotated translation of the Amharic *Andəmta* commentary on Genesis 1:1-2:4—from his personal manuscript collection that he purchased while living in Gondar—all of which is proceeded by the following survey of Ethiopian influencing material: the Biblical, apocryphal, and pseudepigraphic texts, the Commentaries on Genesis, the "Question and Answer books,"[28] the

---

[24] Getatchew Haile, "Review of Ethiopian Biblical Interpretation: A Study in Exegetical Tradition and Hermeneutics," by Roger W. Cowley, *Journal of the Royal Asiatic Society of Great Britain and Ireland.* (1990), 378.

[25] Cowley *op. cit.,* 6.

[26] Ibid., 2.

[27] August Dillmann, *Biblia Veteris Testamenti Aethiopica, in quinque tomos distributa* (Fr. Chr. Guil. Vogelii, 1853). Although useful, this critical edition is lacking in precision, see Haile, "Review of Ethiopian Biblical Interpretation," 379.

[28] Exegetical texts written in question-and-answer format.

Hexaemeric literature, *The Book of the Mysteries of Heaven and Earth*,[29] the homilies and miracles, the chronographic works, the Ethiopic *Qälemənṭos*,[30] the *Gädlä Adam wä Hewän*,[31] and Miscellanea.

In like manner, Chapter 5 examines the theme of Christology with an annotated translation of the Amharic *Andəmta* commentary on Hebrews 1, patristic quotations of the chapter, and its Ge'ez text.[32] All proceeded by the following survey of related Ethiopian material: material associated with the text of the Epistle to the Hebrews in biblical manuscripts, commentaries on Hebrews, creeds and other liturgical texts, patristic works other than commentaries, theological tracts, refutation of heresies, parts of the *Andəmta* corpus, and modern works.

In Chapter 6, titled "Hermeneutical Implications of This Study," Cowley concludes that the Ethiopian exegetical tradition is in essential continuity with Antiochene exegesis[33] and has been molded into its present form by

---

[29] For an English translation see Bakhayla Mîkâ'êl, *The book of the mysteries of the heavens and the earth and other works of Bakhayla Mîkâ'êl (Zôsîmâs)*, trans. E. A. Wallis Budge (Berwick: Ibis Press, 2004). For a Ge'ez manuscript see EMML 2161, ff. 2a-101b.

[30] The Book of Clement as in EMML 2147, ff. 3a-124a.

[31] For an English translation see. Solomon Caesar Malan, *The Book of Adam and Eve, Also Called the Conflict of Adam and Eve with Satan, a Book of the Early Eastern Church, Translated from the Ethiopic, with Notes from the Kufale, Talmud, Midrashim, and Other Eastern Works*, (London: Williams and Norgate, 1882).

[32] Compared to manuscripts found the British Library, one of which exists in digitized form as B.L. Or. 526.

[33] Cowley is of the opinion here that the Antiochene school, as represented by St. John Chrysostom is understood as being concerned with moral application of the Scriptural text. It is in this way he says, that

Ethiopian scholars to elucidate the text and not with inclinations towards doctrinal or theoretical hermeneutics.

Sister Kirsten Stoffregen Pederson's[34] (1932-2017 CE) book titled *Traditional Ethiopian Exegesis of the Book of Psalms* (1995) was submitted for a doctorate at the Hebrew University of Jerusalem. It begins with an introduction that summarizes characteristics of the commentary tradition along with its technical terminology, its role in the worship of the Ethiopian church, and a survey of published works on the traditional exegesis of the book of Psalms—in Greek, Latin, Syriac, and Arabic. Chapter 1, titled "The Ge'ez Psalm Titles," is a study of the titles of the Psalms in the Masoretic text, the LXX, in ancient Jewish and Christian commentaries, and the *Andəmta* commentaries. Chapter 2 "The Ge'ez Text of the Book of Psalms as It Appears in the *Andəmta* Edition" examines how the Ge'ez text closely follows the LXX, with what terminology the *Andəmta* lists variant readings, a list of variant textual readings in the Psalms, and a look at the three instances in the commentary on Psalms where the opinion of *Sedi Pawlos*[35] is recorded. Chapter 3, "The Amharic *Tərgʷame*

---

the Ethiopian tradition resembles the Antiochene school of interpretation.

[34] Sister Pederson was a member of the Ethiopian Orthodox *Täwahədo* monastic community in Jerusalem, see Alehegne, *Ethiopian Commentary on the Book of Genesis*, 15. She was deeply tied to the Ethiopian community in Israel and Ethiopia, "Dr. Kirsten Stoffregen-Pedersen," *The Ecumenical Theological Research Fraternity in Israel*, n.d., http://www.etrfi.org/stoffregen--pedersen-dr-kirsten.html.

[35] *Sedi Pawlos'* identity is still a riddle, what is clear is that he is a foreigner, Pederson *op. cit.,* 45.

Dawit" is the main body of the work and contains the commentary on various Psalms[36] with English translations. In her final chapter, "Hermeneutical and Exegetical Implications of the Study," she confirms without a doubt the Antiochene connection that Cowley wrote about by showing that most of the commentary on the Psalms is drawn from Theodore of Mopsuestia. She finishes this section by summarizing the interpretive methodology as applying direct literal translations of the Ge'ez text into Amharic, illustrative stories, question and answers, grammatical remarks, alternative interpretations, referring to textual variants, geographical information, and Ethiopianizing of material by applying Ethiopian proverbs and similia.

Pederson's last contribution *The Amharic Andəmta Commentary on the Abraham Stories Genesis 11:24-25:14* (1997) is like her previous work, but much shorter. Here, within nine pages she shows how the Ge'ez text follows the LXX, presents technical terminology of the *Andəmta* corpus, and summarizes the methodology in the same manner as before. She then examines the commentary on the Abraham stories which are presented completely in English translation. She also concludes that the commentators are interested in the immediate, direct understanding of the text and not in a typological or mystical interpretation, she is therefore of the opinion that "they are closer to the *nätäla tərg^wame* (simple interpretation) than to the *mesṭir tərg^wame*,

---

[36] Psalms 1, 4, 13, 34, 43, 49, 71, 77, 109, 131, and 151.

a clarification based on the meaning without too much attention to the words."[37]

Miguel Angel Garcia adds a synchronic study aimed at complementing the diachronic works of Cowley and Pederson titled "Ethiopian Biblical Commentaries on the Prophet Micha" (1999). The work has three sections; the first is "Methodological Remarks and Sources" and contains a description of eight manuscripts on the commentary of Micah. The second part, "Literary Form and Technical Terminology of the Commentaries on the Prophet Micah," is written to add to the current description of technical vocabulary that has thus far been described. He asserts that this has not been sufficiently studied by previous works which limited themselves to simply listing the technical terms found within the commentary. Garcia on the other hand aims to elaborate on the terminology and the literary form associated with it. He does this by analyzing the literary form of the commentaries and studying the function and localization of technical terminology in his manuscripts. The third part, "Critical Edition and English Translation of Ethiopian Commentaries on the Prophet Micah", is the main object of the research and contains the text-critical edition of the commentaries of Micah with English translation.

Andəmta as an Interpretive Strategy: with Reference to the Book of Genesis (2003) is an M.A. thesis by Mersha Alehegne submitted to the Addis Ababa School of Graduate Studies. The research aims to provide a starting point for the

---

[37] Pederson, *op. cit.*, 261.

study of the *Andəmta* techniques of interpretive strategy for those studying Amharic literature. This includes a discussion of the recurring introductory material at the beginning of a book, the commentary pattern, the recurring *andəm* for additional commentary, the illustration with a story (*tarik*) or with a quote (*ṭəqs*), the explanation (*hätäta*); among other, related information.

Another work by Mersha Alehegne is his doctoral contribution to the University of Hamburg titled "The Ethiopian Commentary on the Book of Genesis: Critical Edition and Translation" (2011). The main body of the work is a text-critical edition of the commentary on the book of Genesis, which is found in Chapter 2 with an English translation in Chapter 3. These are preceded by introductory material in Chapter 1 where he discusses the history of the commentary tradition with a significant focus on the oral history surrounding it, as told by the indigenous scholars. Although much of this oral history does not stand up against objective data, it is still important in examining the thought-world of the tradition and therefore contains much ground for philosophical examination.[38] In this same section is a table that summarizes the current state of publication of the commentary texts[39] in addition to some discussion on the "upper house" (*lay bet)* and the "lower house" (*tačč bet)* schools of interpretation, the former of which is extinct.[40]

---

[38] Much of Ethiopian literature can be hyperbolic, mythical, or apocalyptic and a balanced approach is necessary.

[39] The publication of the commentary texts was first initiated by Ras *Täfäre Mäkonən* before he became Emperor Haile Selassie.

[40] These styles will be discussed in full detail in Chapter 3 of this study.

Mersha's work is important in this study for its information on the Ge'ez text of Genesis and its commentary, in addition to the information it contains on the state of publication of *Andəmta* texts and its summarization of the traditional Ethiopian perspective.

Adding to the studies of theological motifs and sources is *The Metamorphosis of Satan in the Ethiopic Andəmta Tradition: Historical Analysis of the Possible Sources of Genesis 3:5* (2014) submitted to St. Vladimir's Orthodox Theological Seminary by Gabriel Teshome Alemayehu discusses how the Ethiopian commentators viewed the Serpent and Satan as two distinct entities. He also examines the question of possible foreign sources throughout the Ethiopian Literary periods. Additionally, he explores this notion considering the Ethiopian Christological[41] controversies as the Ethiopian scholars parallel Satan's metamorphosis with the Incarnation of the Logos.

Symbolic Interpretation in Ethiopic and Early Syriac Literature (2017) is a revised version of Ralph Lee's doctoral thesis at London's School of Oriental and African Studies. It provides a section titled, "*The Andəmta Corpus: History and Method*" as a subsection under Chapter 2, which is titled "*Surveying the Ethiopic and Early Syriac Sources*" where he provides a concise summary of primary sources, dating, and exegetical approaches. He identifies Theodore of Mopsuestia's name in the corpus as መሠፍቃን (*mäsafəqan*)

---

[41] See footnote 1.

stemming from the Syriac *məphaššeqānā* "interpreter." Additionally, Ralph Lee has a book chapter called "The Classic *Andəmta* Commentaries on Selected Canticles" in Chapter 5 of *The Songs of Africa: The Ethiopian Canticles* (2017) where he provides English translations of commentary on the first song of Moses (Exodus 15:1-19), Jonah's Prayer (Jonah 2.2-11), the prayer of Azariah (Daniel 3:26-44), and the prayer of Mary (Luke 1:46-55).

Finally, he has an article "The Ethiopic 'Andəmta' Commentary on Ethiopic Enoch 2 (1 Enoch 6-9)" (2014) which presents an English translation of the commentary on Enoch 6-9 showcasing the commentary's view of the fallen angels as holy men who fell into temptation, reflecting the strongly ascetic views of Ethiopian Christianity. Additionally, he discusses the commentary on Psalm 82 and locates a view found in the *Midrash ha-Gadol* but clarifies that nothing conclusive can be said about sources or their routes at the time.

Conclusion

Within 21 years (1967 – 1988 CE) Roger Cowley laid the foundations for the academic study of the *Andəmta* in a way that encompassed both the breadth and depth of the tradition. Beginning with linguistic studies on classical Amharic, surveying the commentary corpus, examining its contents, identifying and tracing the trajectory of its literary influences, and studying its theological motifs and insights into Ethiopian history while searching through its biographical clues to identify the authors themselves.

Cowley's work was that of exploring the mind, heart, and soul of the Ethiopian biblical commentary tradition as well as a search for a hermeneutic philosophy. After Cowley, several others have taken up peripheral studies of the tradition and have contributed to some sections of the field.

These other scholars have provided translations, critical editions, surveys of the literature, and thematic studies. Some have even done so while remaining true to the living tradition, not as a dead specimen to dissect and disseminate. Rather, their work is in unity with the life, thought, eschatological purpose, and mystical sensibility of the texts.

It is here in Cowley's steps that this study aims to pick up, building further on his works and that of others. This endeavor begins with a claim that there in fact exists a hermeneutic axiom at the heart of the *Andəmta* tradition. This contribution towards the hermeneutic questions of the *Andəmta* will be in continuation of Cowley's final work and it will be established through the Biblical theology and linguistic philosophy of the early Church—beginning from circa 300 CE—via the relationship of the Divine Person and the capacity of language. This interpretive philosophy as evidenced within the Ethiopian tradition will be brought to life through the words of the Ethiopian masters and the literary data found within their commentary. It will be compared to similar works from the early Church.

The worldview of the Ethiopian masters found in the oral tradition and folklore will be balanced with other types of historical evidence to harness the life of this tradition. This is done to present a paradigm that has philosophical, theological, and cultural integrity. The paradigm constructed here is suggested as a framework for others engaging in Ethiopian studies, to allow the tradition itself to speak, revealing its mind. This, as opposed to being the object of Western academic interpretation where it is examined through a lens foreign to itself.

Additionally, primary evidence will also be used to reconstruct some picture of a fascinating period of Ethiopian history—16th-18th century CE—and to contribute to the biographical studies by showing something of what the Ethiopian scholars' lives looked like, what their societal contributions were, and the scholarly effort it took to construct the commentaries. Finally, through a particular commentary on Genesis, we will see their view of the theology of suffering to contribute to the previous thematic studies.[42]

---

[42] For example, Cowley's study of the themes of Christology and Creation.

Chapter 2

The Early Church & Variants in the Septuagint[43]

The very first body of work preserving variant readings of the Scriptures is the Hexapla[44] a text-critical tool produced by the 3rd century Church. This period in the history of Christianity and Judaism was already a time when numerous translations of the Scriptures already existed.[45]

The version of the Old Testament used by a significant portion of the early Church was the LXX, a Hebrew to Greek translation made before the Christian era. This was not the only version found among the different Christian communities. For example, the Syriac-speaking Church had its own translation, the Peshitta, a Hebrew to Syriac translation. Regardless, it was the Greek LXX text that would be the focus of the early Church's first text-critical work.

---

[43] The Septuagint will be referred to as the LXX in this study. In the Ethiopian tradition, it is also known as *The Translation of the Elders.*

[44] The Hexapla was the first piece of critical work ever undertaken on the text of the Old Testament and all subsequent work of the kind relied on it. Jerome studied it at Caesarea; the text was later destroyed in the sixth century and only a part of it exists today. Jean Daniélou, *Origen*, trans. Walter Mitchell (Eugene: Wipf and Stock, 2016),136.

[45] The scope of this study warrants caution in discussion the variety of canonical lists. This avoidance should not be confused with an oversimplification of Biblical canon.

The existence of controversies regarding the accuracy of Greek versions of the Old Testament was one of the factors that gave rise to the Hexapla. The LXXs versions in particular contained divergences from Greek versions used among Jewish communities.[46] During the 2nd century CE, Jewish communities began to abandon the usage of the LXX[47] as the doctrinal divide between Christians (a new Jewish sect itself) solidified. During this time the rabbis produced a new Hebrew text[48] and there also emerged several other Jewish Greek translations (those of Aquila, Theodotion, and Symmachus).[49] With the emergence of so many new translations, a clear dilemma emerged which would serve as the driving force for a text-critical tool that preserved different readings of the Old Testament texts.

Variant Readings in the Hexapla

In its physical presentation, the Hexapla was a version of the Old Testament consisting of six columns.[50] There was a column for the Hebrew text,[51] for the LXX, and columns for the Greek texts of Aquila, Theodotion, and

---

[46] Ibid, "Hexapla", in *Early Christian*, 281.
[47] Daniélou, *Origen*,134.
[48] Ibid.
[49] Ibid.
[50] Moreschini and Norelli, "Hexapla," in *Early Christian*, 281.
[51] Whether the first column of Origen's original was a Hebrew text is debated by some. The Hexapla is entirely lost, it is with Eusebius' witness (who consulted it in the library of Caesarea) (*Hist. eccl.* 6.16) that P. Nautin argues the position that Origen most likely did not have the first column in Hebrew, but rather a transliteration of the Hebrew, see *Origene: Sa vie et son oeuvre* (Paris: Beauchesne, 1977), 303-71, in Ibid, 282.

Symmachus. Aquila's translation was very verbally exact and was influenced by the Palestinian rabbis, Symmachus' was like that of Aquila's but was fixated on preserving meaning, while Theodotion's was closer to the LXX and did not differ greatly.[52]

In addition to the six columns, there were also text critical grammar signs[53] used to show the differences between the LXX and the other versions. Therefore, the Hexapla would have been a text-critical tool for understanding the Old Testament to the most exact reading possible. The highlight of its focus on textual exactness would be reflected via the grammatical tools under which variant readings were preserved.

We can see how Origen used variant readings in the Hexapla with the following example. The text of Jerimiah 15:10 contains differences between the LXX and the Hebrew, and Origen says of it that, "there are two readings … we must of course explain the familiar reading used everywhere in the Church [i.e., the LXX], but that does not mean that the one found in the Hebrew texts should be passed over without a word."[54] By this we see exactly how the variant readings were used by Origen to further understand the Scriptures. Variants were preserved for interpretation in addition to the primary reading; this would lead to a more precise understanding.

---

[52] Harry M. Orlinsky, "The Columnar Order of the Hexapla," *The Jewish Quarterly Review* 27.2 (1936), 137–49.

[53] Origen used the obelisk and the asterisk in the same way as grammarians in Alexandria used in their textual criticism of Homer. See Daniélou, *Origen*, 35.

[54] Origen *Comm. Jer.*, 14,3 as quoted in Daniélou, *Origen*, 137.

Origen's LXX column and the collected variants—minus the full text of the other columns—would be copied into future manuscripts of the LXX, with the variant readings being preserved within the margins of later manuscripts. Usually, these later versions of the LXX did not include Origen's text-critical signs, except for the Syro-Hexapla. The Syro-Hexapla is the Syriac rendering of the LXX column including the text-critical signs,[55] and is important to this study as a direct influence on the Ethiopic exegete discussed in Chapter 4.

Textual Epistemology of the Early Church

Encountering differing texts of Scripture raises questions regarding the efficacy of the written word as a vehicle for Divine revelation. Variations in the wording of sacred texts bring about the question of how the textual variants are to be understood. The capacity of language to convey Divine revelation is reflected by the exegetes of the early Church who engaged in these text-critical studies. Starting with Origen,[56] we see that he gathered the 'correct'[57] and variant readings, considering both to be

---

[55] Alison G. Salvesen, "Syro-Hexapla," *Gorgias Encyclopedic Dictionary of the Syriac Heritage: Electronic Edition* (n.d.), https://gedsh.bethmardutho.org/Syro-Hexapla.

[56] Origen was born in 185 CE in Alexandria, ordained a priest in Jerusalem in 230 CE and died in Caesarea (or Tyre) in 254 CE. He lived a remarkable life and we are historically well informed of him, with Eusubius' account as our main source (his account is well established but not without an element of hagiographical legend), "Origen," in *Early Christian,* 269.

[57] Origen aimed at correcting the LXX to draw it closer to the Hebrew exemplar texts, but he was also aware that differences in the Greek could

objects of exegesis.[58] Viewing language as a vehicle for revelation, and not constraining revelation to human (linguistic) mechanisms allowed him to work towards a more accurate reading of the text without being scandalized over differences that exist among manuscript versions.[59] This understanding recognizes the Divine revelation as loftier than the human mechanisms used to carry it, such as words and thought.[60]

This capacity for language is seen in the same way by many Biblical exegetes of the time, not just Origen. St. Ephrem the Syrian and other patristic figures taught that describing God (in explicit language) is reflective of an underlying assumption that the human intellect can "contain" Him, which Ephrem considered erroneous.[61]

---

go back to variants in the exemplars, Ibid, 283. He labored to come as close to an original text as possible, but he retained the variant readings. He says that "I settled the difficulty by consulting the other versions and bringing the passages in question into line with them. When I found a passage that was not in the Hebrew, I marked it with an obelus, as I did not dare to omit it altogether. In other cases, I put an asterisk to show that the passage was not in the Septuagint but was in the Hebrew text and had been added from other Greek versions," Daniélou, *Origen*,135.

[58] Matthew J. Martin, "Origen's Theory of Language and the First Two Columns of the Hexapla," *The Harvard Theological Review* 97, no.1 (2004): 99–106.

[59] There is much speculation regarding Origen's primary aim at compiling the Hexapla, it has been for some, an ideologically neutral source of text-critical data, and for others a polemical tool against Judaism's claim on Scripture. Regardless, a primary motive was surely to use the Hexapla to better understand the Scriptures, Ibid, 99.

[60] Ibid, 103.

[61] Other major patristic figures that wrote about revelation's linguistic transcendence are Sts. Gregory of Nyssa and Gregory of Nazianzus. See Saint Gregory of Nyssa's concept of *diatema*, Matthew Baker, "He Has Clothed Himself in Our Language: The Incarnational Hermeneutic of

Ephrem understood creation and Creator as existing on separate sides of the ontological chasm—a chasm between the two kinds of beings.[62] One illustration of this chasm in the mind of Ephrem is found in the parable of the Rich Man and Lazarus (Luke 16:19-31), across which "what is made cannot reach its Maker."[63] Ephrem finds that symbolic language is necessary to attain a knowledge of God, he describes an essential inadequacy in all human words that speak of God, even those of Scripture.[64] Therefore, he even saw biblical phrases as needing to be read in a way that points away from the words themselves—i.e., avoiding textual literalism—and toward the ineffable reality of God, who can be known and experienced in His Personhood, but not comprehended, defined, or confined to text, thought, or speech.

To this effect Ephrem says that "He clothed Himself in our language so that He might clothe us in His *mode of life*."[65] This expresses that the words of Scripture are intended to convey a revelation to humanity, which is meant to bring humanity into a spiritual modality. The intent of the phrases and wording within Scripture to him was not for purposes of hyper dogmatization; rather, the narratives of Scripture function to show how the Creator is encountered

---

Saint Ephrem the Syrian," *What Is the Bible?: The Patristic Doctrine of Scripture*, ed. Matthew Baker and Mark Mourachian (Minneapolis: Augsburg Fortress Publishers, 2016), 36. Sebastian Brock, *The Luminous Eye: The Spiritual World Vision of Saint Ephrem the Syrian*, Revised edition. (Kalamazoo: Cistercian Publications, 1992), 26.

[62] Ibid.
[63] Ibid.
[64] Baker, *Patristic Doctrine,* 41.
[65] Brock, *The Luminous Eye*, 60.

by the created. Ephrem further elaborates the linguistic mechanisms of this revelation saying "He [thus] spoke with our childish state,"[66] for it is our "metaphors that He put on—though He did not literally do so"[67] since "metaphor does not apply to His true being because that Being is hidden, He has depicted it by means of what is visible."[68] Ephrem describes language as a utility whose functionally is to depict the hidden Being who speaks through language, as one speaks to a child through modes of expression which are accessible to children. These expressions could hardly be called language, but instead, an interaction of persons supplemented by primal expressions due to the limitation of the lesser. It would be erroneous here for the lesser to confine the greater to the confines of these verbal expressions, rather, the expressions function to bind the two persons in relation, in self-revelation.

Ephrem says that in this way the Divine Being spoke to humanity, by expressions that were immediate and comprehendible, although those very expressions are inapplicable to the Godhead. Ephrem viewed language as a necessary means by which to approach knowledge of God but this understanding was balanced out by opposition towards any excessive literalist and rationalistic use of language regarding the Divine.[69]

---

[66] Ibid.
[67] Ibid.
[68] Ibid.
[69] Baker, *Patristic Doctrine*, 41-43.

This same limit on the capacity of rationalism (and the language that expresses it) is discussed in detail by St. Gregory of Nazianzus in his 2nd Theological Oration (Oration 28) where he makes clear his point: the incomprehensibility of the Divine Deity to the human mind.[70] St. Gregory elaborated on the limitations of intellectual pursuits and marveled with Paul the apostle at the depth of God's law, i.e., the wisdom within it.

All truth, all philosophy, to be sure, is obscure, and hard to trace out. It is like employing a small tool on big constructions, if we use human wisdom on the hunt for knowledge of reality [...] our minds cannot receive direct and sure impressions [...] Paul tries to get there—I do not mean to God's nature (that he knew to be quite impossible) but only to God's judgements. Paul found no way through, no stopping-place in his climb [...] the marvel of it all [...] the wonder at the sort of things he (Paul) calls 'the wealth and depth of God' in acknowledgment of the incomprehensibility of God's judgments [...] 'a great abyss' fathomless by sense.[71]

He spoke further of Paul the apostle, who though being advanced in education, preferred at times to simply

---

[70]Gregory of Nazianzus, *On God and Christ: The Five Theological Orations and Two Letters to Cledonius* (Crestwood: St. Vladimir Seminary Press, 2002), 45.

[71] Ibid, 53.

marvel in the apprehension of the divine, instead of engaging in rational thought:

> Let us give [...] much attention to Paul when he says: 'We know in part and we prophesy in part.' This and the like is the confession of one who is no mere layman in knowledge [...] a great champion and teacher of truth. Yet he counts all knowledge in this world as nothing more than 'puzzling reflection in mirrors,' because it has its basis in small-scale images of reality.[72]

According to Origen, those who erred in Biblical interpretation had "failed to find the right way of dealing with the Holy Scriptures,"[73] primarily due to a *literal* fixation on the letter of the text(s).[74] In a homily, he urges Christians to learn the Scriptures with their full faculties, and even to the extent of comparing one text to another.[75] This text-critical philosophy was motivated by an understanding of the limitedness of language and the unlimitedness of the Being who spoke through it.[76]

---

[72] Ibid, 52.

[73] Daniélou, *Origen*, 141.

[74] Particularly Marcion, who rejected the entirety of the Old Testament because he fundamentally erred in his approach to the Scriptures due to literal fixation, Ibid, 143.

[75] *Op. cit.*, 12, 2.

[76] Each variant of Scripture embodies some act of providence. Martin, "Origen's Theory of Language," 103.

What this presents is an epistemology that asserts the Scriptures functioning as a vehicle of revelation without raising the text—in its linguistic qualities—to the capacity of containing the Divine. We see here from Patristic thought that the text is a mechanism of revelation, to be approached with awe, coupled with an understanding of the limited capacity of language, speech, and thought, while yet serving as a mouthpiece for the Divine as He converses with the created in its primal state, urging it on to a higher mode of existence. This shows us how to understand variant readings through a patristic perspective and to appreciate variants as fertile ground for interpretation, allowing for the apprehension of the divine mysteries from differing (variant) perspectives (readings).

Conclusion

The first three centuries were periods in which Christians (a new Jewish sect) and Jewish communities finalized their canon of Scripture. In their process of canonization we see the epistemology of the ancient Church regarding the text of Scripture. This epistemology views the dispensation (οἰκονομία) of revelation regarding the Divine Being as utilizing human language for the sake of mankind. Human language does not apply to the Creator, but He clothes Himself in it for the sake of the created.

Therefore, the language of Divine revelation—which is the text of Scripture—is approached with an emphasis on the content of revelation as sitting on a higher plane over its linguistic elements. At the same time, the text is itself held in such a serious and critical regard that slight variations among different manuscripts are preserved since the linguistic elements are viewed functionally as a vehicle of Divine revelation.

In other words, the textual epistemology of Scripture held by the early Church is text-critical and textually transcendent. This is reflected in the writings of major Church Fathers such as St. Ephrem the Syrian and St. Gregory of Nazianzus and is preserved within the apparatus of Origen's text-critical work. We see variant readings from Origen's Hexapla passed on through later versions of the LXX and thus traversing the topography of the ancient Christian communities. One such version is the Syro-Hexapla whose variant readings have influenced the Ethiopian commentary on Genesis 37:3.[77]

It is important to emphasize here the direct connection between differences among ancient versions of the Scriptures and interpretive positions of ancient communities because every variant reading is in some measure a commentary.[78] Differences in certain readings among texts allow for the traceability of disputed passages, additionally, they shed light on the history of how the passages themselves were understood.[79] In the case of this study, the ancient versions of Scripture that are at play—

---

[77] It is unknown if the Syro-Hexapla exists in Ethiopic, the influence here may have been attained through commentaries that refer to it.

[78] Bruce M. Metzger, *The Early Versions of the New Testament: Their Origin, Transmission, and Limitations* (Oxford: Oxford University Press, 1977), vi.

[79] Ibid.

beyond the Greek versions of the LXX—are those of the Ethiopic, Syriac, and Arabic texts. Moreover, such details speak to the doctrinal, liturgical, and ascetical interests of those who made or used such translations[80] and shed light on the geographical spread of certain variant readings.[81]

Chapter 4 will show how a particular variant traversed the Hexapla to the Syro-Hexapla, and then to the Ge'ez text of Genesis, with an examination of the theological intent of the Ethiopian author.

---

[80] Ibid.
[81] Ibid, vii.

Chapter 3

The Bible in the Ethiopian Church

The Biblical Text in the Ethiopian Church

According to the manuscript evidence, the Ge'ez version of the Old Testament was drawn from Greek versions of the LXX. Some modern academic studies that support this conclusion have been based on the Ge'ez texts of Genesis, Psalms, Esther, and Ezekiel.[82] In addition to Greek, there is evidence of later influence from Hebrew and Syriac.[83]

We know that the translators were diverse in their abilities—some more skilled than others—and belonged to

---

[82] John Russiano Miles, *Retroversion and Text Criticism: The Predictability of Syntax in an Ancient Translation from Greek to Ethiopic* (Chico: Society of Biblical Literature, 1985). Pedersen, Kirsten. "The Amharic *Andemta* Commentary On The Abraham Stories." In *The Book of Genesis in Jewish and Oriental Christian Interpretation A Collection of Essays*, edited by J. Frishman and L. Van Rompay. Lovanii: Peeters Publishers, 1997, 254. Knibb says that the aim of his work is to provide a critical edition of the oldest accessible text of the Ethiopic version of Ezekiel, which is generally assumed to be the text that most closely reflects the Greek *Vorlage*, Michael A. Knibb, *The Ethiopic Text of the Book of Ezekiel: A Critical Edition* (Oxford: Oxford University Press, 2015), 2.

[83] Pedersen, Kirsten. *Amharic Andemta,* 255. Michael A. Knibb, *Translating the Bible: The Ethiopic Version of the Old Testament* (British Academy, 1999), 32.

47

differing periods.[84] The consensus within Ethiopian studies is that these periods of translation—and later, revision—occurred (generally) in three distinct stages of Ethiopian history.[85]

Regarding the Old Testament text, the initial translation from Greek LXX sources seems to have occurred in the period from 4th-7th century CE.[86] Second, the Vulgar Recension where the Old Ge'ez was revised against Syro-Arabic texts is approximated to the 14th century CE.[87] Third, the Academic Recension is dated to the 15th century CE where the revision was in light of Hebrew sources.[88]

The traditional Ethiopian account of scriptural reception differs greatly from the modern historical theory. This legend tells of an ancient Hebrew source from the time of the Israelite King Solomon and is embedded in the psyche of Ethiopians as part of the national myth. It is not the place of legend to refute objective textual evidence, although care must be taken so as not to remain with little more than textual datum.

A proper weighting of insights from both is necessary in literature where subjectivity functions as the

---

[84] Pedersen, Kirsten. *Traditional Ethiopian Exegesis of the Book of Psalms.* (Wiesbaden: Otto Harrassowitz Verlag, 1995), 4.

[85] Knibb, *Ethiopic Version*, 3.

[86] Ibid.

[87] This coincides with the literary renaissance of the restored Solomonic Dynasty, Ibid.

[88] This version of the text is the one found in most of the later Ge'ez Old Testament manuscripts, Ibid.

mode by which the listener/reader is brought into the story. Excessive objectivity here would be nothing more than the shallow mimicking of the scientific method outside of its applicable realm. The importance of legend is especially paramount in Ethiopian studies as well as Biblical studies as it is impossible to understand the literary tradition of either, or even explore the text's narrative absent of its lore. Textual evidence allows us to approach a more accurate reading, map the transmission trajectory, and refine our historical understanding of a text. What the textual evidence cannot do is replace the world that the texts themselves open to us.

This balanced approach is not completely foreign to the *Andəmta* tradition, for evidence we need to go no further than *Mäməhir Kidanä Wäld Kəfle*[89]—circa 1870—to whom we owe the printed edition of the *Andəmta* commentary on Ezekiel. Emperor Haile Selassie summoned *Kidanä Wäld Kəfle* from Jerusalem particularly to undertake this work. Haile Selassie was the impetus for the printing of commentary texts for the first time in Ethiopian history, a work he took up to ease the difficulty faced by those who engaged in traditional ecclesiastical studies.

This commentary on Ezekiel was printed in 1924 and the Scriptural text found in it is based on a Hebrew version of Ezekiel.[90] *Kidanä Wäld Kəfle* also produced a Ge'ez lexicon written with linguistic insights from Hebrew, Syriac, and Arabic. Master (*Mäməhir*) *Kidanä Wäld Kəfle* was a

---

[89] *Encyclopaedia Aethiopica* 3, s.v. "Kidanä Wäld Kəfle."
[90] Ibid.

more recent Ethiopian biblical scholar and his 30-year stay in Jerusalem allowed him to learn Greek, Hebrew, Syriac, and Arabic.[91] Regarding his view of textual transmission, in his lexicon he shows that the Ge'ez text of Scripture was copied from Greek sources. He bases his argument upon morphological evidence found in nouns, comparing them against Hebrew and Greek. He concludes with harsh discourse directed at Ethiopians of the past, including the unknown scribe(s) who wrote a particular hagiography (that of *Qostos*), but his critique is more intensely directed at one of the most prolific and consequential Ethiopian theologians, the monk Abba *Giyorgis*.[92] He criticizes Abba *Giyorgis'* theological compendium the *Book of Mysteries* (*Mätshäfä Mistər*), written in about 1424 CE, for propagating the legend of a Hebrew source text.[93]

አንዳንድ፡የዕብራይስጥ፡ቃል፡ይገኛል፡
ወይ፡ግዕዝ፡ያልተመለሰው፡ቃል፡ጽርኡም፡
ዕብራይስጡም፡ጥሬ፡ይባላል።ጥሬነቱም፡
የቀውስቶስን፡ገድል፡የጣፉ፡ሰዎች፤ይልቁንም፡
አባ፡ጊዮርጊስ፡በመጽሐፈ፡ምስጢር፡
ሰሬዳቸው፡ሳያበጥሩ
ሳያንጠረጥሩ...ዕብራይስጡን፡ብቻ፡ዐፍነው፡
ሽፍነው፡ጠቅሰው፡ታል።እንደዚህ፡ያለው፡

---

[91] Ibid, 399.

[92] Abba *Giyorgis* is also known as *Giyorgis* of Sägla, see *Encyclopaedia Aethiopica* 2, s.v. "Giyorgis of Sägla."

[93] *Mäṣḥafä Säwasäwu wä Mäzəgäbä Qalat Hadis—* መጽሐፈ፡ሰዋሰው፡ ወግስ፡ወመዝገበ፡ቃላት፡ሐዲስ[*Book of Grammar*, Verbs, and Lexicon] (1948), xvii.

ጥቅስ፡ቄርበት፡ነክ፡ምስጢረ፡በክ፡ወይም፡
ማታለያ፡ሽፍጥ፡ገበሬ፡አስደንግጥ፡ይባላል።

There appear to be some Hebrew words that
have not been translated into Ge'ez, these
untranslated Hebrew and Greek are deemed
"unripe" words. The (element of) unripeness is
seen through the scribes who wrote *The
Hagiography of Qostos*, or more importantly, in
Abba *Giyorgis' Book of Mysteries* who failed to
filter (sift) and edit (the unripe words). Instead, he
hid and covered things up, citing only the Hebrew
(purposefully omitting the Greek). The practice of
quoting in such a manner *"seems like a cover up,
a rot of mystery,"*[94] or a "clever attempt to
mislead, startling the simple folk."*[95]

Kedanä Wäld continues scolding the clerics who
propagate legends of an ancient Hebrew source text, in the
following quote he aims at the high priest of Axum Zion St.
Mary's Church (formal title *Nǝburä Id*). He does so
poetically, following a rhyme scheme and using parables as
follows:[96]

ብሉያችን፡በዘመን፡ብሉይ፡
ከዕብራይስጥ፡ተመለሰ፡ማለት ፤በነብረድ፡

---

[94] *Kidanä Wäld* is rhyming here as he slights Abba *Giyorgis'* 'unfiltered'
text, calling it ቄርበት፡ነክ፡ምስጢረ፡በክ.
[95] He says here more literally, 'startling the farmer,' i.e., the honest and
unlettered folk.
[96] Ibid.

ይሥሐቅ፡እጅ፡ሳይከከና፡ሳይበካ፡ሳይ ጋገር፡
ምጣድ፡ሳይ ነ ካ፡እም ኅበ፡አ ልቦ፡የ ተ ገ ኘ፡
የ ሐ ሳ ብ፡የ ም ኞ ት፡የ ሕ ል ም፡እ ን ጀ ራ፡ነ ው።

To say that our Old Testament (the
Ge'ez text) was translated during the Old
Testament period from a Hebrew source is
likened to a piece of dough, unkneaded,
unleavened, unbaked, at the hands of *Nəburä
Id Yəshaq*, a baseless tale, an imaginary and
desirous morsel that one chases in his
dreams.

Kidanä Wäld Kəfle was one of the most erudite
traditional Ethiopian scholars of his time and he labored to
contribute to the body of knowledge. Although he was
respected and admired for his sharp intellect, this opinion on
the sources for the Ge'ez text was not accepted by most
traditional scholars and is probably even unheard of by the
masses of Ethiopian clerics who are far less lettered.[97] As he
says himself, the lack of linguistic caution in handling the

---

[97] The archeologist Enno Littman encountered *Kedanä Wäld* during his
Jerusalem stay in December of 1899 CE. Littman who was passing
through Jerusalem, acquainted himself with several Ethiopian monks and
acquired a manuscript collection from Kedanä Wäld, one was titled *On
the History of Ethiopia* (ታሪክ፡ዘኢትዮጵያ). Enno suggests that *Kedanä
Wäld* was the original writer; he also mentions that he was a poet, which
is surely accurate, as all *Andəmta* scholars must first learn Ge'ez poetry
before they begin Biblical studies. This is also why his insults follow a
rhyme scheme. The snapshot provided by Littman's brief encounter is
that of an erudite and well-read young *Kedanä Wäld*. See, Enno
Littmann, "Abyssinian Apocalypses," *The American Journal of Semitic
Languages and Literatures* 19.2 (1903): 83–95.

translation of certain words leads to a "rot of mystery," or, a corruption of Divine revelation, because it is the language of the text that functions as revelations vehicle.

This goes to show that beyond the modern historical theory, there are essentially two traditional views within the Ethiopian Church. Those who have sided, even in the past, with Greek Old Testament sources, based on textual evidence, and those who derive a textual theory from legends and fables, which have no support from textual data. The latter view is extremely prevalent, even now within the Ethiopian tradition, and it surely does not aid the progress of Biblical studies but is rather a contributor to the "rot of mystery" evident in the chaos of theological dogmas and concepts conveyed by many Ethiopian clergy. *Kedanä Wäld (right) and his teacher Kəflä Giyorgis (left). The title reads: "Orthodox Scholars."*[98]

---

[98] Ibid, ii.

The Medieval Ethiopian Church Context

Sometime around the 17th century, the Amharic *Andəmta* commentary tradition began to crystalize from an earlier Ge'ez *Tərg^wame* tradition.[99] To be clear, the Amharic commentary on Ge'ez text called *Andəmta* is a highly stylized and formulaic tradition, it was preceded by a Ge'ez commentary tradition on Ge'ez text known as *Tərg^wame*, which itself was not stylized or synthesized into uniformity. Both seem to have been influenced to some degree by manuscript marginalia; this is not surprising considering the link between variant readings and interpretive positions discussed in the proceeding conclusion section. Roger Cowley hypothesized that marginal annotations in manuscripts were the core nucleus of the commentary tradition. Cowley concluded this after a short study on a text from 1938, which indeed showed the *Andəmta* commentary—although from a small sample study—had direct verbal correspondence with marginal annotations in manuscripts dating to 1720 CE.[100] As previously mentioned, marginal annotation was also the method by which variants from the Hexapla were incorporated into newer LXX copies, including the Syro-Hexapla.

According to its internal evidence, the definitive formulation and crystallization of the *Andəmta* tradition occurred during the Gonderine line of kings.[101] This

[99] Alehegne, *Ethiopian*, 2.
[100] Roger W. Cowley, "The Beginnings of the Andem Commentary Tradition," *Journal of Ethiopian Studies* 10.2 (1972): 1–16.
[101] Cowley, *Traditional Interpretation of the Apocalypse*, 25-26.

evidence is based on language, historical references to Ethiopian emperors, Ethiopian history, geography, world view preserved in the commentary, and manuscript evidence.[102] The crystallization of the tradition seems to have been tied closely to one particular Gonderine ruler, Emperor Iyasu I the Great, (r. 1682-1706 CE), whose throne name was *Adəyam Sägäd* (lit. to whom the earth bows).[103] Just a little more than a century before him, "the Left Handed" Ahmad b. Ibrahim al-Gazi (1506-1543 CE)[104]—nearly wiped out much of the Ethiopian literature, architecture, and cultural heritage in his jihad against the Christian kingdom.[105]

To remedy this, the Emperor summoned the most talented scholars among the clergy to the new imperial city of Gondar, where he encouraged them to refine and standardize the branches of religious studies.[106] It may have been under his patronage that two newly emerging branches were standardized into uniform studies. Regardless of whether it was due to him, or due to the emperor(s) before him, roughly around this time, the previously existing form of non-eucharistic chant (*Zema*) would develop into another elaborate and captivating non-eucharistic chant (*Aq^waq^wam*), and from the previous Ge'ez commentary tradition (*Tərg^wame*) would emerge a more stylized and formulaic

---

[102] Ibid.

[103] Paul B. Henze, *Layers of Time: A History of Ethiopia* (London: C. Hurst & Co, 2000) 102.

[104] *Encyclopaedia Aethiopica* 1, s.v. "Ahmad b. Ibrahim al-Gazi."

[105] Ibid, 87.

[106] Henze, 102.

Ge'ez/Amharic commentary tradition (*Andəmta*). The patronage of the emperors would ensure their survival and propagation.

The Development of Andəmta: Ethiopian Lore and Historical Evidence

The traditional account of the emergence of Aq^waq^wam paints a picture of the time and place in which the *Andəmta* corpus also developed. The account reveals the ethos of the time, especially among the Ethiopian clerics. By traditional accounts, the momentum for the new forms of chant and biblical commentary was attributed to holy and ascetic hermits tucked away in caves on high mountains. These traditional accounts are in line with historical evidence regarding Ethiopian monastic spiritual and ascetic practices. An example is the 15th-century witness of the Portuguese Pero de Covilhao, who observed the presence of 'many' hermits in 'the great forests' and in 'the greatest depths and heights of the mountains,'[107] which echoes extreme asceticism given the great ruggedness of the land. The legend of $Aq^waq^wam's$ initial development points particularly to a mountain named *Däbərä Hazälo* in the far eastern boundary of the land.[108]

---

[107] Pankhurst, *The Northern and Central Highlands*, 44.

[108] This is between Wello and modern day Harar, See *Mädaləw Aləbab YäAqwaqwam Mələkit*— መዳለው፡አለባብ፡የአቋቋም፡ምልክት [*Treasury of Hearts: The Musical Notation of Aq^waq^wam*] (1991 E.C.), x-xxi.

Here, a few centuries before Emperor Iyasu, it was rumored that angelic songs were revealed to a monk Abba *Mäzmurä Qədusan*, who in turn taught Abba *Esdros*.[109] The hermit Abba *Esdros* left the mountainous seclusion to teach these melodies in the city of *Ankobär,* south of Gondar.[110] He did so until Ahmed's jihad laid waste to the city, at which time Abba *Esdros* moved north towards Gondar,[111] in his later years, he would retire atop a mountain near the city of Gondar.[112] On this mountain, his voice could be heard, but despite searches for the hermit, he was nowhere to be found; Abba *Esdros* had vanished from the material world. The Emperor ordered the scholars of the previously established musical tradition (*Zema*) to listen to the melodies emanating from this mountain. He thus began the development of the *Aq^waq^wam* tradition into a uniform and standardized school of chanting in what was at that time the imperial capital of Gondar.[113] According to the contemporary *Mäməhir Henok*, who was a more recent living member of the tradition[114]

በዚሁ፥ተራራ፥አባ፥አንበስ፥የሚባል፥
ዝጉሐዊ፥ባሕታዊ፥የበቃ፥መነኮሴ፥ይኖር፥
እንደ፥ነበር፥ይነገራል።የአባ፥አንበስ፥ደቀ፥
መዛሙር፥ወይም፥ረዳት፥አባ፥መዛሙረ፥
ቅዱሳን፥ይባላል።አባ፥መዛሙረ፥ቅዱሳን፥

---

[109] Ibid.
[110] Ibid.
[111] *Mädaləw Aləbab*— መዳልወ፥አልባብ [*Treasury of Hearts*], x.
[112] Ibid.
[113] Ibid.
[114] Ibid.

ይኸን፡የበቃ፡መነኮሴ፡በቅን፡በመርዳቱና፡
በማገልገሉ፡ብቃት፡በተሰማው፡ጊዜ፡ዕድል፡
ተርታው፡ጽዋ፡ፈንታው፡አቋቋም፡በመሆኑ፡
እስመ፡ስሙ፡ይመርሓ፡ኀበ፡ግብሩ፡እንዲል ...
በአንድ፡አንድ፡ወዳጆቹ፡እና፡አገልጋዮቹ፡ላይ፡
አድሮ፡ሥራውን፡መግለጽ፡የተለመደ፡ነው፡
ወይም፡ልማዱ፡ነው።መንክር፡እግዚአብሔር፡
በላዕለ፡ቅዱሳንሁ፡ተብሎ፡የሚመሰገንበት፡
ይህን፡በመሰለ፡አምላካዊ፡ሥራው፡መሆኑ፡
ግልጽ፡ነው።አባ፡መዝሙረ፡ቅዱሳን፡
ለባሕታዊ፡ኤስድሮስ፡አስተማረው።ባሕታዊ፡
ኤስድሮስ፡በአንኮበር፡መንግሥት፡አንኮበር፡
ከተማው፡ገብቶ፡ማስተማር፡ጀምሮ፡ሳለ፡
በግራኝ፡ምክንያት፡የአንኮበር፡መንግሥት፡
ፈለሰ።

On the mountain (*Däbərä Hazälo*)
was a holy, recluse, ascetic monk named
Abba *Anbäs*,[115] his disciple and his helper
was called Abba *Mäzmurä Qədusan*. He [the
latter] would aid and assist this monk [the
former] with integrity, and when he [the
latter] had sensed in himself *bəqat*,[116] it came
to pass that his lot in life was to compose the
Aq^waq^wam melodies; as it is said 'for his

---

[115] Abba Anbäs' name implies he lived among lions in the wild.
[116] This essential means implies some level of *theosis*.

name informs his deeds'[117][...] it is customary for the Lord to reveal his deeds through his friends and servants, it is his custom to act in this way. This is the reason for His glorification [accord to the Psalm] 'marvelous is the Lord among his holy ones,' it is because of such deeds. Abba *Mäzmurä Qədusan* taught the hermit *Esdros*, who taught [the melodies] during the rule of *Ankobär*, in the city of *Ankobär*, until the rulers were dispersed due to the Left-handed one.

The oral history recounted here by *Mämhər Henok* paraphrases the period of about (1400 – 1700 CE). It places the hermit *Esdros'* final retirement in the northern city of Gondar from 1530 CE—around the time of Ahmed's attack—to 1682 CE—during the reign of Emperor Eyasu I. Although not an accurate historical source, this oral account sheds light on the ethos of the time, conveying the lived tradition's esteem for learning and ingenuity coupled with godliness and mysticism.

The Portuguese traveler Francisco Alvarez noted the piety of the Ethiopian clergy in 1520 CE for their extreme acts of charity,[118] fasting, vigils, and mortification of the

---

[117] Abba Mäzmurä Qədusan's name means "Songs of the Holy Ones," it is a common belief that names are tied to the essence of the person, and therefore informs their deeds in life.

[118] Pankhurst, *The Northern and Central Highlands*, 3.

body.[119] These erudite and mystic figures were to be found in church schools either within monastic communities, under the patronage of some feudal lord, and in some cases under the patronage of an emperor, or supporting themselves by other means, often in austere conditions.

There were also those of more suspect character who were shrewd and beguiling, especially among those circles within proximity to the imperial court or the nobility, whose favor they would strive for as they meddled in intrigues and plots. These clerics were also extremely talented in their learning. Alverez notes that in some churches the clerics numbered from 400 to 800, with several large churches numbering 4,000 clerics.[120] These men were of great reputation and so fierce in their competition and guile that Emperor *Ləbnä Dəngəl* (circa 1520 CE) had to relocate some 200 from the church of *Mäkanä Səllase* (lit. [dwelling] place of the Trinity) to prevent them from "eating each other up."[121]

In addition to the multitude of Ethiopian clerics were a few very high-ranking characters such as the abbot of *Däbrä Lebanos* monastery who was the head of Ethiopian monasticism (formal title *Eccege*), and the Egyptian Bishop (formal title "the *Abun"*). Around the period leading up to the crystallization process of the *Andəmta* tradition, the monastery of *Däbrä Lebanos* had been laid waste by Ahmed's armies. Therefore, the Abbot may have resided far

---

[119] Ibid, 44.
[120] Ibid, 29.
[121] Ibid, 29-31.

north from the monastery, possibly in the city of Gondar in a compound bordering the Egyptian Bishop's residence known as the *Abun Bet*[122] (lit. House of the Abun). These two figures were the highest ranking among the clergy and were both influential to the rulers of this period.

There were also a small number of Catholic Portuguese missionaries between 1557-1632 CE whose influence was significant.[123] The emperors had established relations with the Portuguese with the desire to advance their kingdom, while the agenda of the Jesuits was to convert the land of Ethiopia to Catholicism.[124] Although small in number the Jesuits had won the support of some of the nobility, they were at odds with the Ethiopian monks and clergy at large.[125] The Jesuits viewed the Ethiopian Church as deteriorating and doctrinally inferior.[126] They practiced rhetoric and persuasion for use in doctrinal debates against the Ethiopian clergy, and to gain favor among the elite.[127] They also engaged in violence when their rhetorical practices failed to produce the desired outcome.[128]

---

[122] *Encyclopaedia Aethiopica* 1, s.v. "Abun Bet."

[123] The first Jesuits landed in Ethiopia in 1557. See Jessica Wright, Leon Grek, and Leonardo Cohen, *The Jesuits in Ethiopia (1609-1641): Latin Letters in Translation*, 1st ed., ed. Wendy Laura Belcher (Wiesbaden: Harrassowitz Verlag, 2017), 1.

[124] It was the dream of Ignatius of Loyola, the founder of the Jesuits (Society of Jesus), to convert the Ethiopians to Roman Catholicism. See Ibid, 1.

[125] Ibid, 2.

[126] Ibid, 5.

[127] Ibid, 6.

[128] Ibid.

In addition to the drama at play among these characters, the empire was weakened by internal strife, war with nomadic tribes, and Muslim conflicts and invasions. During the late medieval period, the church was struggling to preserve its past and nurture the creativity unveiled in the present. This tumult is the context in which we find the beginning of the Amharic/Ge'ez *Andəmta* commentary tradition and its formulation into a uniform interpretive tradition. One of its stylistic qualities especially important in the scope of this study is its preservation of variant readings.

Mäməhir Henok[129]

---

[129] *Mädaləw Aləbab—* መዳለው፡አለባብ[*Treasury of Hearts*], xxi.

Variant Readings Preserved in the Andəmta

The *Andəmta* corpus' commentary flows in groups of literary blocks. These blocks are written in old *medieval* Amharic with stylized technical language.[130] The span of the technical language is wide and for this study it is useful to mention only two which are used by the Ethiopian scholars to critique and correct the Biblical text. The corpus preserves variant readings most explicitly using the technical term *yəlal abənet* [ይላል፡አብነት], effectively meaning "(thus) says a model (text)," or "(thus) says an important source." In the context that we find in this study, *abənet* refers to model texts which are codex manuscripts.[131] It should be noted that this technical term seems to point to variant readings gathered from ancient versions of the Bible. Another technical term that points to alternative readings is the *"sil näw"* [ሲል፡ነው] ("it means to say") which is used to correct the Ge'ez text for a better reading. There are numerous technical terms within the corpus, these are sufficient for the scope of this study.

The structure used here to present a block of commentary will be in the following sequence. First, the chapter and verse of the passage, then the Ge'ez text of that

---

[130] *YäQəddus Pawulos*— የቅዱስ ጳውሎስ [*St. Paul's*], vi. Roger W. Cowley, "Preliminary Notes on the Baläandəm Commentaries," *Journal of Ethiopian Studies* 9, no 1 (1971), 11. Pedersen, *Amharic Andemta,* 255.

[131] Manuscripts in scroll form are often limited to magic spells; most other Ethiopian manuscripts are codices.

passage, followed by its English transliteration, and then the English translation. The Amharic commentary on that verse will follow in a subsequent block, introduced as *andəm* and followed by the Amharic commentary, then its English translation, such as below.

Passage chapter: verse

Ge'ez Text

   English Transliteration

   English translation

andəm

   Amharic commentary

   English translation of Amharic commentary

andəm ...

andəm ...

 The technical terms themselves are located within the blocks of *andəm* commentary, as can be seen in the following examples.[132]

---

[132] Note that this format omits the Amharic paraphrasing (*zäyəbay*) of the Ge'ez text.

Variant Readings in Commentary on the Old Testament

The following is an example where the term *sil näwu* [ሲል፡ነው] ("it means to say") is used to correct the Ge'ez text of 1st Samuel 23:14 for a more accurate reading.

1st Samuel 23:14.

ወነበረ፡ውስተ፡ገዳም፤ገዳሙ፡ዘይት፤

wä-näbärä wustä gädam, gädamä zäyət.

And he (David) remained in the wilderness, the wilderness of *Zäyət.*

andəm.

ዘማሴሬት፡ሲል፡ሰጐን፡የሚታደይንበት፤

it means to say *"zä-masayrayt"* where the ostrich is hunted.

A wilderness is mentioned twice, the commentary clarifies that the first one mentioned by the Ge'ez text is that of *"masayrayt"* a Ge'ez word derived from the Greek *maserem.* The LXX here reads ἐν Μασερεμ.[133] This is originally the Hebrew *mashadot*, whose meaning is, "mountain fastnesses, hunting places."[134] This also echoes the description attached to the second mention of a

---

[133] 1Sa 23:14 LXX.
[134] Roger W. Cowley, "The Beginnings of the Andem Commentary Tradition," *Journal of Ethiopian Studies* 10.2 (1972), 12.

wilderness in that same verse, as "narrow straits," or obstacle ridden passes in the LXX- "ἐν τοῖς στενοῖς."[135]

Additionally, the Ethiopian commentary says that this is the place where the ostrich is hunted, which may be insight derived from geographical knowledge of the Holy Land or it may simply be the recruitment of indigenous imagery from the Gonderine highlands employed by the Ethiopian masters to convey the landscape.[136]

The point here is that the commentary section clarifies that the first mention of a wilderness is that of 'masayrayt,' a reading that is absent from the Ge'ez text which Cowley possesses, but it is present in the original LXX. It should be noted that Cowley's manuscripts are of no textual significance so nothing consequential can be said about their shortcomings.[137] In fact, the standard Ge'ez text of the Book of Samuel shows nothing lacking. Instead it showcases the expected behavior for an exact translation of the LXX—even following word order of the Greek.[138]

- καὶ ἐκάθισεν Δαυιδ ἐν τῇ ἐρήμῳ ἐν Μασερεμ

---

[135] 1Sa 23:14 LXX.

[136] The Syro-Arabian ostrich (*S. camelus syriacus*) became extinct in 1941 CE. See "Ostrich | Habitat, Food, & Facts," *Encyclopedia Britannica*, n.d., https://www.britannica.com/animal/ostrich.

[137] Cowley mentions his manuscripts are limited in value to tracing manuscript marginalia and that they have no textual significance. See Cowley, "Beginnings," 1.

[138] The English translation is mine, the Greek is 1 Sa 23:14 LXX. For the Ge'ez text see Yä Gə'əz Mätəhafə Qəddus—የግዕዝ መጽሐፈ ቅዱስ [The Ge'ez Bible] (Addis Ababa: Ethiopian Orthodox Täwahədo Church, 2021), 320.

ወነበረ ዳዊት ውስተ ገዳም ዘማሴሬት

And David dwelt in the wilderness of Maserem

- ἐν τοῖς στενοῖς καὶ ἐκάθητο ἐν τῇ ἐρήμῳ ἐν τῷ ὄρει Ζιφ

ውስተ መጽብብ ወነበረ ውስተ ገዳም ውስተ ደብረ ዚፍ

In the narrow straights and dwelt in the wilderness of Mt Ziph

What this example shows is the commentary tradition preserving a more accurate reading—taken from an LXX source—under the mechanism *sil näwu* [ሲል፡ነው] ("it means to say"). Additionally, this shows us how the Ethiopian scholars used this mechanism to help a defective text read more accurately.

Variant Readings in Commentary on the New Testament

Below is the prime mechanism for alternative readings, the *yǝlal abǝnet* [ይላል፡አብነት] ("says a model text"), in a New Testament commentary example. The pericope of the Gospel of John 14:16, whose text reads, "And I will pray the Father, and he shall give you another Paraclete, that he may abide with you forever," is presented in the *Andǝmta* as follows:

- **John 14.16**

ወአነ፡እስእሉ፡ለአብ፡ይፈኑ፡ለክሙ፡
ጰራቅሊጦስሃ፡ካልዓ፡ዘይሄሉ፡ምስሌክሙ፡
እስከ፡ለዓለም

wä-anä isəlo lä-abə yəfänu lä-kəmu
praqəleṭosə-ha kalə'a zä-yəhaylu məlaykəmu
isəkä lä-alämə

And I will pray to the Father, that he may send to
you the Paraclete, another helper, who will be with
you unto the end of ages.

andəm.

ለዘላለም፡ከናንተ፡ጋራ፡የሚኖር፡
ጰራቅሊጦስን፡ይልካል።ጰራቅሊጦስ፡ማለት፡
መጽንዒ፣መንጽሒ፣ናዛዚ፡ከሣቲ፡መሥተፍሥሒ።
ካልዓ፡ባልዉ፡አንድ፡ገጽ፡የሚል፡ሰባልዩስ፡ይረታል፤
ዘከማየ፡የሚል፡አብነት፡ይገኛል፡መንፈስ፡ቅዱስ፡
ሕፁፅ፡የሚል፡መቅዶንዮስ፡ይረታበታል

He will send the Paraclete who will live with
you until the end of ages. Paraclete means one
who strengthens, one who sanctifies, one who
consoles, one who reveals hidden things, one who
brings joy. With his word "another" Sabellius who
claimed "one ገጽ"[139] is refuted. There is a model

---

[139] Literally one face, mask or person πρόσωπον.

text that reads "(another) like me" with which Macedonius is refuted.

We see the commentary's doctrinal focus here regarding the personhood of the Paraclete, the Holy Spirit. In that vein, two heresies of the early church are quickly mentioned, that of Sabellius and Macedonius. The commentary mentions that there is a text which reads, "(another) like me" [ሀስማየ] (zä-kämayä), with which Macedonius' heresy is refuted. What is interesting here is that this reading is noted as a variant from an important text, but such a source is absent among the different manuscript families of Ge'ez John,[140] according to the critical edition of the Ge'ez text of John.

The manuscript families represented in the critical edition span all the important Ethiopian literary periods, but none contain this variant reading.[141] Interestingly St. John Chrysostom's (circa 370 C.E.) commentary on this verse references Sabellius, in addition to mentioning that the text is worded "Another like Me,"[142]

> [...] that is, 'Another like Me.' Let those be ashamed who have the disease of Sabellius, who hold not the fitting opinion concerning the Spirit. For the marvel of this discourse is this, that it has stricken down

---

[140] M. G. Wechsler, *Evangelium Iohannis Aethiopicum Aeth. 109* (Louvain: Peeters Publishers, 2005), 89.

[141] See the manuscripts cataloged in Ibid, ix-xiv.

[142] John Chrysostom, *Homily 75 On The Gospel of John*, https://www.newadvent.org/fathers/240175.htm

contradictory heresies with the same blow. For by saying 'another,' He shows the difference of Person, and by 'Paraclete,' the connection of Substance.

Two key points are shared by both Chrysostom and the Ethiopian commentary, the reading, "like Me", and the mention of Sabellius, but the third point—mention of Macedonius—seems to be missing.

Further examination shows that Chrysostom is speaking here about two distinct heresies that are stricken down in one blow, one regarding the Substance and another regarding the Personhood of the Holy Spirit. Therefore, it seems that the issue of Substance was understood correctly by the Ethiopian scholars as Pneumatomachianism and therefore the direct mention of Macedonius was added in the *andəm* block.

If we look further at the Greek text, it reads ἄλλον παράκλητον (another Paraclete) with ἄλλος (another) meaning, "another of the same kind"[143] as opposed to ἕτερος, "another of a different kind"[144] and it seems highly likely that this insight was gained from Chrysostom's commentary. But if this was the case, what was the Ge'ez source for Chrysostom's commentary on John?

Identifying the sources that the *Andəmta* scholars used is often complex, which is also the case in this instance

---

[143] "Strong's Greek: 243. Ἄλλος (Allos) -- Other, Another," n.d., https://biblehub.com/greek/243.htm.
[144] "Strong's Greek: 2087. Ἕτερος (Heteros) -- Other," n.d., https://biblehub.com/str/greek/2087.htm.

since the Ethiopian church does not have a printed edition of the commentaries of John Chrysostom. Some of Chrysostom's commentaries do appear in small fragments in *The Faith of the Fathers* (*Häymanotä Abäw*), an 11th century florilegium translated into Ge'ez during the reign of Emperor Gälawdeos, and was printed in 1974 CE.[145] The section containing some of Chrysostom's works does not seem to be a source for his commentary on John 14.

Other possible sources that contain commentary tracts by Chrysostom, like the Book of Hawi (*Mätshäfä Hawi*) are unprinted and exist in codex formats such as the 247-folio codex found in the British Library collection BL Or. 779. Although the Book of Hawi contains fragments of Chrysostom's commentary on the Gospel of John in general and parts of chapter 14, more work is needed to pinpoint its influence.[146]

This example shows how a variant reading preserved by the *andəm* tradition can point to texts beyond those represented locally and whose influence can be from a broad array of ancient Christian works which cite authoritative and ancient Biblical manuscripts.

---

[145] Siegbert Uhlig, ed., "Häymanotä Abäw," in *Encyclopaedia Aethiopica* (Wiesbaden: Harrassowitz, December 1, 2005).

[146] I was able to pinpoint some folios in BL Or. 799 where Chrysostom's commentary is quoted from chapter 14 of John's Gospel, but they did not contain the desired verse.

Variant Readings in the Commentary of the Book of Monks

The next example is from *Mar Yəshäq*, one of the three ascetical texts contained in the Ethiopian collection of the *Books of Monks* (*Mäṣḥāftä Mänäkosat*). This text is attributed to Isaac of Nineveh (7th century CE) but is in reality comprised of three separate texts: most of the 'First Part' of the original Syriac writings of Isaac, in addition to four homilies by Yohannan of Dalyatha (8th CE),[147] and an abbreviated version of the Letter to Patricius by Philoxenos of Mabbug (5th CE).[148]   The Ge'ez text of *Mar Yəshäq* appears to be a 15th-century Arabic to Ge'ez translation of Abu l-Fath 'Abdallah b. al-Fadl of Antioch's 11th-century text,[149] the *Andəmta* refers to him as *Gäbərä Egəzi'abəher* ("slave of God" i.e. Abdallah) *Wälədä Fadəl* (**ገብረ፡ እግዚአብሔር፡ወልደ፡ፋድል**).[150] The translation from Arabic

---

[147] Also known as Yohannan Saba ('Elder'). He was an East Syrian monk and mystic, writer of mystical discourses, letters, and maxims. Brian Edric Colless, "Yoḥannan of Dalyatha," *Gorgias Encyclopedic Dictionary of the Syriac Heritage: Electronic Edition* (n.d.), https://gedsh.bethmardutho.org/Yohannan-of-Dalyatha.

[148] Aaron M. Butts, "Ethiopic Christianity, Syriac Contacts With," *Gorgias Encyclopedic Dictionary of the Syriac Heritage: Electronic Edition* (n.d.), https://gedsh.bethmardutho.org/Ethiopic-Christianity-Syriac-contacts-with. Bishop of Mabbug, he was an "ascetic theologian, Christological polemicist and sponsor of the Philoxenian NT." David A. Michelson, "Philoxenos of Mabbug," *Gorgias Encyclopedic Dictionary of the Syriac Heritage: Electronic Edition* (n.d.), https://gedsh.bethmardutho.org/Philoxenos-of-Mabbug.

[149] *Encyclopaedia Aethiopica* 3, s.v. "Isaac of Ninevah."

[150] *Mar Yəshäq* — **ማር ይስሐቅ** [*Isaac of Nineveh*] (*Täsəfa Gäbərä Səlasay* Press, 1982 E.C), 1.

to Ge'ez seems to be the work of a monk by the name of
Sälik (late 16th century) of *Däbərä Libanos*,[151] the *Andəmta*
records that it is unknown who translated *Mar Yəshäq* into
Ge'ez but that some say it was *Sälik* of *Däbrä Libanos*.[152]
The commentary of interest is found in the 6th homily of the
1st chapter, the section titled "On the Excellence of
Meekness Over Championing in Debate"[153] (በእንተ:ዘከመ:
ይኄይስ የውሃት:እመነ:ተጋዕዛ).

Mar Yəshäq 1:6

ይኄይስከ:ይብሉሉከ:ዓማፄ:በእንተ:ሕፀፀ:
አእምሮትከ:እምትኩን:ተዋሣኤ:
ወመስተጋዕዘ:ኢየሀልዩኬ:በእንቲአከ:ከመ:አንተ:
ጠቢብ:በእንተ:ድፍረትከ ወኢጋሬሮትከ።

*yəhayisəkä yəbilukä amaṭse bänətä hətsätsä
aəmərotikä imətikun täwasa'ay*

*wä mästäga'izä ehäləyukay bäinteakä kämä antä
ṭäbebə bäintä dəfrätəkä wä-ehafrotəkä*

It is better that they might say of you 'he is a
rebel' because of the faultiness of your
understanding rather than being [acceptable to
them as] one who is conversant and a

---

[151] *Encyclopaedia Aethiopica* 4, s.v. "Sälik."

[152] *Mar Yəshäq* — ማር ይስሐቅ [*Isaac of Nineveh*], iv.

[153] The numbering is of course according to the Ethiopic text, which does
not seem to correspond to the numbering in other versions of Isaac of
Nineveh's homilies, Ibid, 14.

debater. Let them not think that you are
wise through boldness and shamelessness on your
part.

andəm.

ይትሀለይ፡ብከ፡ይትበሃል፡ብከ፡ይሃልይ፡ብከ፡
ይበሉከ፡ይላል፡አብነት፡፡ትርጓሜው፡አንድ፡ነው፡፡
ደፍረህ፡ተከራክረህ፡ተከራካሪ፡አስቸጋሪ፡የተየከሽ፡
መላሽ፡ኪሉህ፡አላዋቂ፡ቢሉህ፡ይሻላል፡፡

 'it will be thought of you' (yətəhäläy bəkä),
'it will be said of you' (yətəbähäl bəkä), 'they
will think of you' (yəhäləyu bəkä), 'they will say
of you' (yəbəlukä), <u>says a model text</u>, the
interpretation (regardless of the variants) is one
and the same. It is better for them to say of you,
'he is ignorant' than for them to say, 'he is a
debater, troublesome, and a returner of debts
[i.e., returner of evil]' by way of zealous debate.

The Ethiopian commentary preserves four variant
readings here which are deemed inconsequential, and their
interpretation "is the same." This set of four grammatically
equivalent variants points to differences in local manuscript
versions available to Ethiopian scholars.

The manuscript families represented in the critical
edition of the Ge'ez text of *Mar Yəshaq* contain none of these
variants, instead, one different variant is preserved,

እምነየስh[154] which is witnessed by two manuscripts, only one of which is dated to the 17/18th century.[155] Any critical edition intends to provide a more accurate reading of a text by critiquing it against the best manuscripts, this is of course a text-critical methodology, and the presence of numerous variants in the *Andəmta*—as seen in this and previous examples—surely asserts it as a text-critical tradition.

Regardless, unlike the Ge'ez Old and New Testaments, it is hard to imagine this text being constantly edited against more authoritative versions since it is an instructional text, not a dogmatic one. Additionally, its translation seems to have occurred relatively later in Ethiopia's literary history as compared with the text of the Bible. Of course, this argument relies on the dating of the text to be around the 16th century; which is a reasonable conclusion given the influx of Oriental Christian texts somewhere between 1500-1600 CE, in addition to some of the characters of *Däbrä Libanos* monastery who we know actively translated Arabic texts.[156] But to be clear, it is the commentary tradition that approximates this date, it is not

---

[154] Dawit Berhanu, *Das Mashafa Mar Yeshaq von Ninive. Einleitung, Edition und Übersetzung mit Kommentar*, 1st edition. (Hamburg: Verlag Dr. Kovac, 1997), 41.

[155] EMML 15 has been estimated to be of 17/18th century origin according to its catalog which also states that it was awarded to the church of St. Marks (*Qəddus Marəqos*) of Addis Abeba in 1924 CE. The other manuscript EMML 734 does not have an estimated date.

[156] Chapter 6 discusses how Emperors *Gälawdeos* and *Susenyos* and some of the learned monks of *Däbrä Libanos* engaged in translating Oriental Christian texts.

information gleaned from a study of the text in its literary qualities or its manuscript evidence.

The Old Testament example shows us that the text was continually critiqued against better sources, and we see the paraphrasing of the text in the commentary corrects it to read more accurately. The New Testament example shows evidence of variant readings collected from the commentary of early Christian sources foreign to Ethiopia. Finally, the example from the Book of Monks shows that variant readings may also point to differences in local manuscript copies. Roger Cowley had previously concluded much of the same, that the variants preserved are indeed textual variants whose sources are not mentioned,[157] minus one instance of a reference to the "Shoa Gospel" and another to *"Yared's* Text."[158]

The above examples singularly show and collectively assert that the *Andəmta* scholars were critiquing the text upon which they were commenting. They would do so by relying on various sources, some native, and others from the Christian Orient (see Figure 3). The *Andəmta* provides clues but finding its exact sources requires significant detective work.

---

[157] Cowley, *Traditional Interpretation of the Apocalypse*, 57-58.
[158] Ibid.

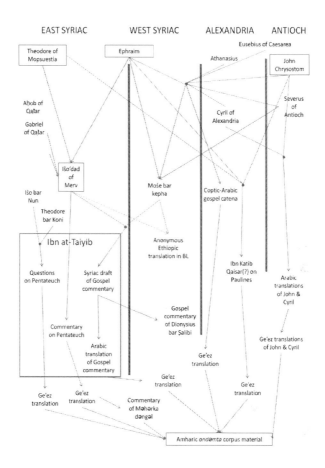

Some Andəmta Sources[159]

---

[159] Originally in Cowley, *Traditional Interpretation of the Apocalypse*, 39. Taken from Ralph Lee, *Symbolic Interpretations in Ethiopic and Ephremic Literature*, vol. 24 of *Eastern Christian Studies* (Leuven: Peeters Publishers, 2017) 48.

The Textual Epistemology of the Ethiopian Church

The fact that the *Andəmta* corpus preserves variant readings is sufficient evidence to conclude that the commentary tradition is not fixated on textual-literalism and that it is in fact a text-critical tradition. It has been shown so far that variants are not simply preserved but are also objects of commentary. This is exactly the text-critical and textual-transcendent epistemology seen in the thought of the prominent early Church exegetes. Approaching these textual differences with the intent to understand the spirit of the written word affirms that Divine revelation transcends the literary and grammatical elements of language. The spirit of the text is seen here going above and beyond its lettering. The language here is not a means to itself, rather, it has a function, to be the vehicle which reveals the Divine Person.

Additionally, this conclusion is further encouraged by one of the few Masters (*Mämhəran*) who is mentioned within the corpus, *Mäməhir Esdros* (circa 1700 CE)[160]—not to be confused with the hermit Abba *Esdros*. This *Esdros* is so consequential to the tradition that his opinions are recorded in the commentary on Luke 2:27, John 5:8, and the commentary on the *Wəddase Mariam* (*Praises of Mary*) 56,

---

[160] The *Esdros* here is not to be confused with the hermit Abba *Esdros* mentioned in the legendary tale of aqwaqwam's development. There is no evidence that these are the same characters; the oral history of their lives is also vastly different.

75, and 81 while remaining almost silent of any other scholars.[161]

He boldly exclaimed that the Ge'ez text of Scripture is defective.[162] According to the oral history he concluded this after having taught in Gondar for a significant portion of his life, after which he retired south to one of the monasteries in the Lake Tana region. During this retirement he examined '600' texts in various churches and monasteries, he subsequently revised the entire tradition with one of his focuses being the editing of Ge'ez Scriptural texts.[163] The traditional Ethiopian scholars say that "*Esdros* preferred to attempt to find a 'better' Ge'ez text as a basis for interpretation, rather than to expend ingenuity on a defective text."[164] It is significant that he stated this in the 1700s which is rather late in Ethiopia's literary history, seeing as how the initial translations of Scripture had commenced 1,200 years prior. What this means is that not only does the medieval legacy show clear signs of a text-critical orientation, but even in more recent times, it is described by its most important scholars as a text-critical tradition.

---

[161] Cowley, *Traditional Interpretation of the Apocalypse*, 25-26.

[162] Alehegne, *Ethiopian Commentary on the Book of Genesis*, 10.

[163] *Esdros* was also unsatisfied with the body of the corpus and his revision was aimed at making the commentary more concise and evenly distributed. Alehegne, *Ethiopian Commentary on the Book of Genesis*, 10.

[164] Roger W. Cowley, "Mämhər *Esdros* and His Interpretations," in *Ethiopian Studies: Proceedings of the Sixth International Conference* (Addis Ababa: Institute of Ethiopian Studies, 1980), 42.

Mämǝhir Esdros' opinions are undeniable and irrefutably important. The entirety of the *Andǝmta* tradition that survives to this day is based on his revised style called *tačč bet* (the lower house), any traditional scholar engaging in *Andǝmta* is a disciple of his. The *lay bet* (upper house) style is extinct, probably due to its lack of refinement and verbosity, qualities which made it difficult to commit to memory. Additionally, it did not put any effort into correcting the Ge'ez text. Even with an acknowledgment of the limitations of the Ge'ez text, it is remembered as avoidant of engaging in text-critical efforts. The oral tradition says the following of a particular "upper house" teacher:

> When he interpreted books, he would take the text as it was read to him, and did not say, "This is an omission, this is an addition." When they asked him why, he would say, "One must interpret as it is read because by reason of translators' errors, the true reading of any books written in Ge'ez is not known." Because of this, his commentary was called the commentary of the upper house.[165]

We have already seen the opinion of *Kidanä Wäld Kǝfle* regarding the Old Testament sources but here it is also

---

[165] The upper house Master remembered here was *Qes ase* (lit. Priest to the King) Gäbrä Mädǝn, Ibid. His name implies that he was confessor to the king of his time.

useful to add *Kəfle's* view of the Ge'ez text, he says the following:[166]

ዐልፎ፡ዐልፎ፡መሥመር፡ይጥላል፤ቃል፡
ይለውጣል፡፡ይህንንም፡ዐብራይስጥና፡ጽርእ፡
የሚያውቁ፡ግእዝ፡የተማሩ . . . ይመስክራሉ፡፡
ጆርመናዊው፡ሊቅ፡ሰዲ፡ጳውሎስም፡ለጎንደር፡
ሊቃውንት፤ትፈቅዱ፡እንደ፡ኸነ፡ብሉያትችኹን፡
ከዐብራይስጥ፤ሐዲሳትችኹን፡ከጽርእ፡
እያስማማኹ፡ዐርሜ፡ንባቡን፡ከነትርጓሜው፡
አሳትሜው፡ብዙ፡መጸሕፍት፡ላምጣላችኹ፡
ቢላችው፡አንፈልግም፡ብለው፡በምቅኘንት፡
እንዳስቀሩት፤ቅንነት፡ያላችው፡ብዙ፡ሰዎች፡
ይተርኩታል፡፡   ርሱም፡በታሪኩ፡ጥፎታል፡
ይባላል፡፡

Here and there the Ge'ez text fails (to convey) the mystery (of revelation). This is well known by anyone who knows Hebrew, Greek, and Ge'ez, [...] they will tell you. The German scholar Sidi Pawlos[167] told the scholars of Gondar that if they were willing, he would edit their Old Testament against

---

[166] *Mäṣḥafä Säwasäwu wä Mäzəgäbä Qalat Hadis*— መጽሐፈ፡ሰዋሰው፡ ወግስ፡ወመዝገበ፡ቃላት፡ሐዲስ [*Book of Grammar, Verbs, and Lexicon*] (1948), xvii.

[167] Sidi Pawlos was a visitor who seems to have lived among the scholars of Gondar, he is one of the few people mentioned within the corpus. He is recorded as suggesting corrections to the Ge'ez text of Psalms, see Cowley, *Traditional Interpretation of the Apocalypse*, 32.

Hebrew, and their New Testament against Greek texts, in addition to the commentary. They told him they were unwilling; it was out of spite.[168] There are many witnesses who in uprightness will tell the truth of this story, it is also said that Sidi Pawlos wrote about this history also.

Kəfle describes the occurrence of textual issues "here and there" within the Ge'ez text. He also mentions that this occasionally results in its inability to convey the divine mystery. This shows here, as it did in the case of the ancient Church, the understanding of revelation as loftier than the linguistic mechanisms which carry it, which is exactly what is conveyed by *Kəfle*. In addition, *Kəfle* rebukes the *Andəmta* scholars who had assembled in Gondar during his time because they had knowledge of the limitations of the Ge'ez text but failed to resolve these issues, "out of spite."

In all fairness, the Gonderine scholars would not have had the amount of exposure to different languages and sources which *Kəfle* had. It should not be forgotten that *Kəfle* had a vast cultural exposure due to his stay in the Holy Land in the 1800s where he would have met peoples from nearly all Christian dispensations. This would have only broadened his already wide linguistic and literary proficiency. It should not be a surprise that those scholars in Gondar would be suspicious of Europeans, they would have had reason enough just from the memory of the experiences with the

---

[168] Alternatively, out of jealousy.

Jesuits. Therefore, the strife between *Kəfle* and the scholars assembled at Gondar is expected.

Regardless, *Esdros'* and *Kəfle's* were not the only opinions, surely the most popular—i.e., the most common— opinion is that the text is beyond criticism. One can even observe this attitude among present-day Ethiopian clerics who contend with each other in doctrinal debates over defective texts. But it is the epistemology of the *Andəmta*, in continuity with the ancient Church and those fruits which must be relied on, not the sentiments of the masses.

Conclusion: A Core Hermeneutic "The Letter Kills & the Interpretation Gives Life"

All of this seems to be summed up in the commentary on 2 Corinthians 3:6. The Ge'ez text of this verse reads, "for the *book*[169] kills, but the Spirit gives life." In 2 Corinthians, the Apostle Paul briefly contrasts the Old and the New Covenants and connects the Law with sin/death and the Gospel with the Spirit/life. The *Andəmta* conveys this as the first interpretation and follows up with another of a hermeneutic concern.[170]

---

[169] The Ge'ez text preserves the reading as "book" (*mäṣhaf*), which should be understood here as "writing(s)." The Greek preserves "letter" (γράμμα), which is itself to be understood as "Scriptures," or "writings." See "Strong's Greek: 1125. Γράφω (Graphó) — to Write," n.d., https://biblehub.com/greek/1125.htm

[170] *YäQəddus Pawulos—* የቅዱስ ጳውሎስ [*St. Paul's*], 207.

2 Corinthians 3:6

እስመ፡መጽሐፍ፡ይቀትል፡ወመንፈስ፡
ያሐዩ

*əsmä   mäṣhaf   yəqätəl   wä   mänəfäs
yəhäyu*

for   the   writings   kill   and   the   spirit
gives life

andəm.

ሕገ፡ሥጋ፡ኦሪት፤ይጎዳልና፤አኮ፡በሕገ፡
መጽሐፍ፤ሕገ፡ነፍስ፡ወንጌል፤ይጠቅማልና፡
አላ፡በሕገ፡መንፈስ

The law of the flesh, the Torah, brings
harm; 'not by the law of the writings.' The
law of the spirit, the Gospel is beneficial,
'instead by the law of the Spirit.'

andəm.

ንባብ፤ይጎዳልና፤አኮ፡በሕገ፡መጽሐፍ፤
ትርጓሜ፤ይጠቅማልና፡አላ፡በሕገ፡መንፈስ

The letter brings harm; 'not by the
law of the writings.' The interpretation is
beneficial, 'instead by the law of the Spirit.'

The Ethiopian scholars understand Paul's contrast
between the Law/death and the Spirit/life as also the contrast
between the letter of the Law which can lead to death and its
correct understanding which leads to life. Said another way,

the text, if correctly followed, leads to the Divine Being (who is the source of Life). The Ethiopian commentary is reminiscent of Jesus' response in Matthew 22:29 "you err, not knowing the Scriptures, nor the power of God." Uttered to the Pharisees—masters of the Law—asserting that knowledge of the letter of the Law does not necessarily lead to the Divine Being, or what He speaks through it—*for the letter kills, but the interpretation gives life.*

Chapter 4

Məhərka Dəngəl's Commentary

Introduction

All that has been said so far is sufficient preparation to examine a particular medieval Ethiopian commentary on Genesis 37 found in the codex of the Ethiopian Manuscript Microfilm Library project titled EMML 2101.[171] This text has unique qualities that show direct influence from the Syro-Hexapla and the variants allow us to see how the text was understood and interpreted by a particular Ethiopian scholar of the 17th century.

This commentary is of the *Tərgᵂame* genre—Ge'ez commentary upon Ge'ez text—and its influence on the *Andəmta* commentary of Genesis 37 will also be examined. Particularly interesting is that the *Andəmta* commentary's text of Genes 37:3 has been modified in conformity to its commentary on that pericope. This is unlike the three examples studied in the previous chapter, where variants are maintained within the commentary where they are used to correct the reading of the Ge'ez text from the confines of the commentary section. Here the variant rises from the

---

[171] Getatchew Haile, *A Catalogue of Ethiopian Manuscripts Microfilmed for the Ethiopian Manuscript Microfilm Library, Addis Ababa, and for the Hill Monastic Manuscript Library, Collegeville, Vol. VI: Project Numbers 2001-2500* (Collegeville: Hill Monastic Manuscript Library, 1982), 195.

commentary section to edit the actual letter of the text and is therefore a perfect culmination of a study regarding the relationship between the letter (of the text) and its spirit. An examination of this literary data will be preceded by a quick investigation of the author and his one other known work. The title of the commentary is *The Commentary of the Pentateuch* (*Tərgʷame Orit*), and the author is *Məhərka Dəngəl,* meaning Captive of the Virgin (Mary*).*

Məhərka Dəngəl Life and Education

Məhərka Dəngəl was born in 1540 CE and died sometime after 1633 CE past the age of 93.[172] He received his education from Enbaqom, the Abbot of *Däbrä Libanos* monastery sometime before the latter's death in 1560 CE. His teacher, the Abbot Enbaqom himself was a mystic and surely one of the most learned individuals of the time, a native Arabic speaker who also knew Ge'ez and is mentioned as having proficiency in Portuguese, and also, to some lesser extent Coptic, Syriac, Hebrew, Armenian, Latin, and Italian.[173] *Məhərka Dəngəl* himself refers to his teacher as "the virtuous, sage of many texts, and father of many languages"   (ትሩፉ፡መይነ፡መጸሕፍት፡ወአበ፡ልሳናት).[174]

---

[172] *Encyclopaedia Aethiopica* 3, s.v. "Məhərka Dəngəl."

[173] Some of his linguistic acumen is listed in his hagiography, others are mentioned by individuals who encountered him such as Pero da Covilaho and Francisco Alvarez with whom he practiced Portuguese, likewise he is noted as exercising Coptic and Syriac with the Egyptian Metropolitan, *Encyclopaedia Aethiopica* 2, s.v. "Enbaqom."

[174] EMML 2101, f. 148b.

These merits along with his prolific writing,[175] translating of Arabic Christian texts, in addition to his spirituality and devotion are what propelled Abbot Enbaqom—as a native Yemeni—to be the first and only non-Ethiopian ever elected as the head of *Däbrä Libanos* monastery.

In 1613 CE, Məhərka Dəngəl was about 73 years old, some 50 years after the death of his teacher. At this time, during the rule of Emperor *Susenyos*, he held several of the highest offices possible, as the Emperor's teacher, confessor (*näfsə abbot*), and chronicler.[176] In fact, in 1613 CE he was succeeded by another chronicler, regardless he was still in close quarters with the Emperor.[177] He may have stepped down due to advanced age yet between 1613-1614 CE historical records place him as a participant in the Christological controversies as an early supporter of the Two Births (*Hulät Lədät*) doctrine.[178] Moreover, in the absence of Abuna Simon II, the Egyptian Metropolitan of that time, *Məhərka Dəngəl* covered his role of *Abun* amidst the council.[179]

---

[175] In 1540 CE Enbaqom wrote the *Anqätsä Amin*, a refutation of the Quran using its own internal themes against it, this composition is understood as being directed at Ahmad the Left-Handed. See *Encyclopaedia Aethiopica* 2, s.v. "Enbaqom."

[176] *Encyclopaedia Aethiopica* 3, s.v. "Məhərka Dəngəl."

[177] *Encyclopaedia Aethiopica* 2, s.v. "Enbaqom."

[178] The "Two Births: formula is now a core doctrine in the Ethiopian Orthodox *Täwahədo* Church, *Encyclopaedia Aethiopica* 2, s.v. "Enbaqom."

[179] The Kings Christological Council was called to address the controversies that were raging in Ethiopia at that time. The fact that *Məhərka Dəngəl* covered the role of the *Abun* has implications to his importance and erudition, it also speaks to the negligence of the *Abun*.

By the time *Məhərka Dəngəl* had finished his service as the imperial chronicler, he had written the first 22 chapters of *The Chronicles of Susenyos*. This itself speaks directly to *Məhərka Dəngəl's* talent since this office required a "high intellectual caliber that could have been obtained only through merit, free from any inheritance or lineage of the nobility's class."[180] Those who were chosen for this position were "well-established traditional scholars [...] who had advanced knowledge of church education and who were skilled in calligraphic writing, knowing much of Christian literature."[181] *Məhərka Dəngəl's* substantial knowledge of Christian literature is thoroughly established in his work "The Commentary on the Pentateuch" (*Tərg*^w*ame Orit).*

Məhərka Dəngəl's Chronicle Chapters

The first 22 chapters of *The Chronicles of Susenyos* are his only other known works besides his commentary. Even in chronicle writing, the Ethiopian literary tradition is heavily influenced by Biblical style, therefore, similes

---

See Jessica Wright, Leon Grek, and Leonardo Cohen, "Excerpt from the Annual Letter of the Province of Goa, 1613," in *The Jesuits in Ethiopia (1609-1641): Latin Letters in Translation*, 1st ed., ed. Wendy Laura Belcher (Wiesbaden: Harrassowitz Verlag, 2017), 75–91.

[180] Solomon Gebreyes Beyene, "The Tradition and Development of Ethiopic Chronicle Writing (Sixteenth-Seventeenth Centuries): Production, Source and Purpose," in *Time and History in Africa*, ed. Alessandro Bausi, Alberto Camplani, and Stephen Emmel (Milano: Centro Ambrosiano, 2019), 149.

[181] Ibid.

referring to Biblical characters are quite common.[182] The assimilation of one character to another is used in the Biblical text to introduce a new character by comparison to a well-known one, enabling the introduction of the lesser known through the well-established.

An example of this occurrence can be found in the Old Testament writings of 1st and 2nd Kings where kings are categorized as "good" according to their assimilation with the figure of King David.[183] Similarly Ethiopian chronicle writers used this approach to introduce new characters against biblical figures. For example, in *The Chronicle of King Gälawdewos* the Portuguese military are referred to poetically as the "Children of Tubal" (ደቂፀ፡ቶቤል) effectively conveying their craftsmanship (Genesis 4:22).[184]

Similarly, Emperor *Susenyos* is introduced in the 1st Chronicle via two groups of similes: 1) Jacob's son Joseph, then 2) the three youths along with Daniel. This is significant since the remaining chapters preserve accounts of battles and deeds which are inconsequential to a study of Ethiopian Biblical hermeneutics.[185] These similes precede the narrative to establish a hermeneutic pattern, so that the emperor's fortunes and misfortunes are correctly interpreted

---

[182] Dale Allison, "Jewish Figures," in *The New Moses: A Matthean Typology*, (Eugene: Wipf and Stock, 2013), 11–96.

[183] 1 Kings 3:14, 9:4, 11:4, etc., see also Allison, "Jewish Figures", 12.

[184] Solomon Gebreyes Beyene, "The Chronicle of King Gälawdewos (1540–1559) : A Critical Edition with Annotated Translation" (Staats- und Universitätsbibliothek Hamburg Carl von Ossietzky, 2016), 105.

[185] The remaining chapters of the Chronicles of *Susenyos* are important to anyone interested in the dynamics and history of the different tribes, and other issues such as Christian-Muslim relations.

by the audience. The Ge'ez text of the chronicle reads as
follows,[186]

ቅድመኒ፡ተዓውቀ፡ኃይለ፡ረድኤቱ፡
በዮሴፍ፡ወልደ፡እስራኤል፡እምድኅረ፡ተሠይጠ፡
ወኮነ፡ገብረ፡ኮነ፡እግዚአ፡ወመኮንነ፡በምድረ፡
ግብጽ፡፡ዳግመኒ፡ተጠየቀ፡በሠለስቱ፡ደቂቅ፡
አናንያ፡ወአዛርያ፡ወሚሳኤል፡ውሉዱ፡ለኢዮአቄም፡
ንጉሠ፡ይሁዳ፡፡ወዳንኤል፡ወልደ፡እኁቶሙ፡
ለዕሌሆሙ፡ሰላም፡፡እምድኅረ፡ፄወዎሙ፡
ወወሰዶሙ፡ንጉሠ፡ባቢሎን፡ኮኑ፡መኳንንተ፡
ወሥሉጣነ፡ላዕለ፡ምድረ፡ባቢሎን፡እስከ፡ድኅኑ፡
እምእቶነ፡እሳት፡ዘይነድድ፡፡ወእምአፈ፡አናብስት፡
መሣጥያን፡እንዘ፡ይከድኖሙ፡ረድኤቱ፡
እግዚአብሔር፡ክቡር፡ወልዑል፡፡ወይሴውሮሙ፡
እምእከያተ፡አሕዛብ፡መምለክያነ፡ጣዖት፡እስከ፡
አዕረፉ፡በክብር፡፡ወለዝንቱ፡ንጉሥ፡ሱስንዮስ፡
ከደነቶ፡ረድኤተ፡እግዚአብሔር፡ክቡር፡ወልዑል፡
ብዙኃ፡ጊዜያተ

Previously the power of His aid was
known through <u>Joseph the son of Israel</u> after
he was sold and became a slave, he (then)
became lord and ruler in the land of Egypt.
Again, this was confirmed through the three
youths, <u>Anania, Azariah, and Mesial</u>, sons of

---

[186] Translation is mine.   See Francisco Maria Esteves Pereira and
Sociedade de Geografia de Lisboa, eds., *Chronica de Susenyos, rei de
Ethiopia* (Lisboa: Imprensa Nacional, 1892), 5.

Joachim King of Judah and Daniel who was the son of their sister, peace be upon them. After their captivity and after the King of Babylon took hold of them they became rulers and masters in the land of Babylon to the point of being saved from a fiery furnace which burned. They were covered from the mouths of snatching lions with the help of God who is glorious and majestic. And he hides them from the evils of the Nations who are worshipers of idols until they rest in glory. And also this king *Susenyos* was also aided and covered many times with the help God, who is glorious and majestic.

The comparison with Joseph is used to convey *Susenyos'* childhood exile and subsequent rise to authority as part of Divine Providence. His comparison with the three youths and Daniel portrays the honor and dignity *Susenyos* held even when exiled as a child among the "Gentiles."[187] Since the chronicler aims to justify the King's right to rule, points of royal pedigree, divine election, military might, and religious devotion are the primary themes.[188] Therefore the hermeneutic pattern aims to redirect the audience to interpret the King's misfortunes not as points of weakness but as coinciding with the pattern of God's elect. The pattern is that

---

[187] This refers to some of the non-Christian tribes amongst whom *Susenyos* lived as a child captive.

[188] Beyene, "Ethiopic Chronicle Writing," 146.

which is revealed in the religious memory of the relationship between God and mankind as textualized in the Scriptures.

A curious style of writing is evident in the phrase "peace be upon them" which is odd for an Ethiopian and shows *Məhərka Dəngəl's* familiarity with Arab customs. Also, in this same quote we see a viewpoint that Daniel was related to the three youths.

Məhərka Dəngəl's Commentary on the Pentateuch

His commentary titled *Tərg^w ame Orit* 'The Commentary on the Pentateuch' was written in 1610 CE,[189] three years prior to the King's Christological Council. The commentary begins first with an introduction, where, after mentioning the name of Moses and other Old Testament figures, we see again the phrase "peace be upon them."[190] There is also a discussion here on the origin of the Pentateuch and other ancient writings,[191] including a summary of the structure and themes of the text.[192]

ᚃክፍላት፥ዘውእቶን፥ትርጓሜ፥
ወምዕዳን፥ወትንቢት፥፨ወጸሎት፥ወአኰቴት፥
በከመ፥ከፈለ፥ሙሴ፥መጸሐፍቲሁ፥ᚃክፍላት፥

---

[189] Getatchew Haile's catalogue entry states here that the date 1603 is in *Amätä Məhrät* and 1610 in *Anno Domini*. EMML 2101, 196.

[190] This occurs several times just in the introduction, EMML 2101, f.63a-b.

[191] He goes at some significant length about how the Torah was not the first piece of literature in the ancient world and that the ignorant propagate such fables. He refers to the Greeks, Egyptians, Syrians, and Indians, and speaks on astronomy and the naming of celestial bodies in some of those ancient works, Ibid, f. 64a.

[192] Ibid.

ዘዉእቶሙ፡ፍጥረት፡ወፀአት፡ወሌዋዉያን፨
ወኍልቍ፡ወዳግም፨

The 5 (categorical) divisions are commentary, instruction, prophecy, prayer, and praise. In the same way Moses divided the text in 5 sections, Genesis, Exodus, Leviticus, Numbers, and Deuteronomy.

What follows is a flowing commentary on the content of the five books of the Pentateuch. This commentary is vast, containing about 170 folios with three columns per folio.

Mentioned in the colophon is his use of Ge'ez and Arabic as sources material.[193]

ተፈጸመት፡ትርጓሜ፡መጽሐፈ፡ኦሪት፡
ዘአስተናበሮ፡ወአሠነዮ፡እምዐረቢ፡ወግዕዝ፡
ምስኪን፡ምህርክ፡ድንግል፡ወልደ፡ትምህርታ፡
ለደብረ፡ሊባኖስ፡ወረድኦ፡እንባቆም፡ትሩፍ፡
መመይነ፡መጻሕፍት፡ወአበ፡ልሳናት፡
ዘሜጦሙ፡ለብዙኃን፡አሕዛብ፡እምአምልኮ፡
ጣዖት፨ወአቀበ፡ትምህርታ፡ለቤተ፡ክርስቲያን፡
ያዕቆባዊት

Completed here is the commentary on the Pentateuch which was compiled and edited from Arabic and Ge'ez by *Məhərka Dəngəl* the lowly, born of the school of

---

[193] Ibid, f. 148b.

Däbrä Libanos. He was aided by Enbaqom the virtuous, sage of many texts, and father of many languages, who returned many Gentiles from idol worship and guarded the teachings of the Jacobite Church.

His mention of help from the Abbot *Enbaqom* could mean that he used *Enbaqom's* Ge'ez translations of Arabic sources, or, that *Enbaqom* taught him Arabic. If indeed this text was completed in 1610 CE, the Abbot *Enbaqom* would have been deceased already for 40 years. Interestingly he refers to *Enbaqom* as the guardian of the Jacobite Church, and not the Coptic.[194]

Məhərka Dəngəl's Sources

The sources that *Məhərka Dəngəl* used were initially identified by Roger Cowley who first pointed out that this commentary has made use of an Arabic or Ethiopic version of the *Paradise of Christianity* (*Firdaus an-Nasraniya*)[195] by

---

[194] Both *Məhərka Dəngəl* and his teacher, along with the Emperor *Susenyos* show consistent desire and effort to break away from Egyptian ecclesiastical leadership and align with the Syrian church. The details regarding the strained relationship between the learned Ethiopian clergy and the Egyptian Metropolitan is so paradigmatically intriguing that I hope to present it in a separate work. It seems even that the desire of the Emperor to convert to Catholicism during this period is based on the aim of independence from the Coptic Metropolitan who was unable to keep up with the needs of the lettered clergy. Regardless, the Metropolitan was strongly support by the peasantry.

[195] Cowley notes that the author "made use of the commentary of Ibn at-Taiyib as represented in Arabic by MS. Vat. Arab. 37 and in Geez by

Ibn at-Taiyib (d. 1043 CE).[196] The commentaries of Ibn at-Taiyib made their way into Ethiopia sometime in the 16th century and may be one of the several Christian Arabic texts that Emperor *Gälawdeos* paid to have translated in his efforts to remedy the literary decline resultant of Ahmad's destruction. The Abbot *Enbaqom* himself may have been translating these texts which Emperor *Gälawdeos* purchased, or he may have acquired them another way. Regardless, this source was controversial and evidence exists—EMML 7122[197]—attesting to the controversy of Ibn at-Taiyib's messianic interpretations. The exegetical issues that Ibn at-Taiyib's commentaries caused were not unique to him, rather they are characteristic of his East Syrian, or pejoratively 'Nestorian' predecessors.[198] Due to these

---

B.N. d'Abbadie 28." See Cowley, *Traditional Interpretation of the Apocalypse*, 38.

[196] Priest, exegete, physician, philosopher, translator; he worked in a hospital in Baghdad, modern day Iraq and was secretary to the Bishop. Among his most significant works is his commentary the Paradise of Christianity. Aaron M. Butts, "Ibn Al-Ṭayyib," *Gorgias Encyclopedic Dictionary of the Syriac Heritage: Electronic Edition* (n.d.), https://gedsh.bethmardutho.org/Ibn-al-Tayyib.

[197] EMML 7122 f. 51a, col. 1 and Roger W Cowley, "A Ge'ez Document Reporting Controversy Concerning the Bible Commentaries of Ibn At-Taiyib," *Rassegna Di Studi Etiopici* 30 (1984): 5–13.

[198] This influence can be traced directly to Theodor of Mopsuestia's interpretation of messianic figures. The *Andəmta* corpus knows Theodor as መሠፈቃን (*mäsafəqan)* stemming from the Syriac *məphaššeqānā,* or "interpreter." See Ralph Lee, *Symbolic Interpretations in Ethiopic and Ephremic Literature,* vol. 24 of *Eastern Christian Studies* (Leuven: Peeters, 2017), 46. Theodore of Mopsuestia commentary is the main source for the *Andəmta* on the Psalms, see Kirsten Pedersen, *Traditional Ethiopian Exegesis of the Book of Psalms* (Wiesbaden: Otto Harrassowitz Verlag, 1995).

controversies, Ibn at-Taiyib's name is often modified and Ethiopianized to deflect negative attention.[199]

A linguistic study by Aaron Butts built further on Cowley's previous work, it showed how Syriac biblical commentaries were compiled and translated into Arabic by Ibn at-Taiyib in his commentary and finally into Ge'ez in *Məhərka Dəngəl's* work.[200] It particularly identifies the sources influencing *Məhərka Dəngəl's* commentary on Genesis 37:3, one of which is the Syro-Hexapla.[201]

The text of Genesis describes Joseph's tunic, which his father Jacob made for him, as "a tunic of many colors" (Genesis 37:3). The Hexaplaric variant on Genesis 37:3 records that the tunic had four colors.[202] In *Məhərka Dəngəl's* commentary he adds to this multicolored coat, an opinion that it was also embellished with gold embroidery. Another probable source for the tradition regarding golden embroidery is the Ethiopic History of Joseph, a text that was also translated into Ethiopic from Arabic, the Arabic itself was compiled from Syriac sources.[203] Looking at the

---

[199] ቀሲስ፡ክቡር፡አባ፡ፍሥሐ፡ገብረ፡እግዚአብሔር፡ወልደ፡ሥናይ see EMML 1839.

[200] Aaron M. Butts, "Embellished with Gold: The Ethiopic Reception of Syriac Biblical Exegesis," ed. Hans-Georg Beck, *Oriens Christianus. Hefte für die Kunde des christlichen Orients* 42.1 (1956): 409–10.

[201] It shows how Isho'dad of Merv's commentary was incorporated into the 1st part of the Paradise of Christianity which eventually found its way into the *Commentary on the Pentateuch*, Ibid.

[202] Red, black, green, and blue. Ibid, 144.

[203] Kristian S. Heal, "Identifying the Syriac Vorlage of the Ethiopic History of Joseph," in *Malphono W-Rabo d-Malphone Studies in Honor of Sebastian P. Brock* (Piscataway: Gorgias Press, 2008), 205–10.

Andəmta commentary on Genesis 37:3 and its incorporation of both the tradition of 4 colors from the Hexapla, and the tradition of gold embroidery; the question must be asked, what was the source for the *Andəmta*. Was it the Hexapla, Ibn at-Taiyib, *Məhərka Dəngəl*, or the Ethiopic History of Joseph?[204] This question will be addressed shortly.

The Andəmta Commentary on Joseph's Tunic

Turning now to the *Andəmta* commentary on Genesis 37:3, the expected reading is "a tunic of many colors," but something different is preserved in the *Andəmta* scholar's text.[205]

Genesis 37.3

ወገብሮ፡ሎቱ፡ክዳነ፡ዘሕብረ፡ዐሥቅ

wä-gäbro lotu kedanä zä-həbrä osəq

and he made for him an embroidered tunic.

andəm.

ይህም፡ይታወቅ፡ዘንድ፡ōት፡ጎብር፡ᵭኛ፡ ወርቀዘቦ፡ያለዉ፡ልብስ፡አሥርቾልት፡ነበረ

Regarding this (Jacob's love for Joseph), he made for him a tunic <u>of 4 colors</u> and a fifth which was <u>a stripe of gold</u>.

---

[204] This question was original posed by Aaron M. Butts, see Butts, *op. cit, 144*.

[205] Alehegne, *Ethiopian Commentary on Genesis*, 294.

The Ge'ez text here is unusual; it has been edited, not by the Hexaplaric variant (a garment of four colors) but by the tradition of gold embroidery, specifically only mentioning embroidery in the text and omitting 'golden.' Meanwhile, in the body of the commentary, both the Hexaplaric variant and the tradition of gold embroidery are present.

Returning to the previous question of influence, it is suggested here to be of *Məhərka Dəngəl's* doing. The *Andəmta* tradition is aware of his practice of embroidering garments, this requires us to assign more weight to this conclusion than to others. This is a very fortunate example of an individual mentioned by name in the Ethiopian commentary tradition. The *Andəmta* commentary on Matthew 23.5 says the following of *Məhərka Dəngəl*.[206]

ቄስ:አጼ:ምህርካ:ድንግል:ኢየሱስ:ናዝራዊ:
ብለው:በልብሳቸው:ጽፈው:እንደነበረ::

In the same way that the King's confessor *Məhərka Dəngəl* embroidered 'Jesus the Nazarene' on his garment.

Finally, there are three *Andəmta* manuscripts that elaborate more on this embroidery—in the commentary not in the text—one says the golden embroidery was made up of "designs of trees" (ዛፍ:የተቀረጸበት), the other two say it

---

[206] *Wänəgayl Qədus Nəbab KänäTergʷame*—ወንጌል ቅዱስ ንባቡ ከነትርጓሜው [*The Gospel Text with Commentary*] (Addis Ababa, 1992), 243.

was of "vines and budded flowers" (ሐረግ፡የተሳበበት፡አበባ፡ የፈነዳበት).[207]

Categorically speaking, this example represents an ancient variant collected from foreign commentary ascending the *andəm* comment section to edit the Ge'ez text. This shows how some of the scholars would labor to better understand and improve the Biblical text. Here the letter of the text is modified to better articulate the mystical understanding, but what is so significant about Joseph's garment?

Joseph's Embroidered Tunic

The *mämhəran* did not engage the text out of mere curiosity and the focus on Joseph's garment is deeply consequential in understanding the anthropology core to the Scriptures. The relationship between clothing and the person is metaphysical in the Semitic mind, which is the culture in which the Scriptures were written.[208]

Genesis recalls the falling away of humanity, where Adam and Eve were stripped of their "garments of glory," a story that conveys a loss of identity. Their subsequent action, covering their nudity with makeshift coverings, speaks of replacing this lost identity with an inferior one. This anthropological theology of clothing is not a view that has

---

[207] Two of the manuscripts containing this reading are in libraries in Addis Ababa and the third belongs to the *Mädəhane aläm* School of Commentary in Gondar, see the critical apparatus in Alehegne, *op. cit, 144.*

[208] Brock, *The Luminous Eye,* 85-97.

been imposed on the text by the Ethiopian scholars, rather, it is a view that is implicit within the text. The understanding of Adam and Eve's garments as robes of glory is traced to the Rabbis;[209] a tradition that reached Oriental Christians, who in their Semitic minds easily cleaved to the text's original function.[210]

The New Testament proposes that in the "fullness of time" this lost identity was redeemed through the incarnation of Christ,[211] in this vein the Pauline teachings speak of "clothing oneself with Christ"[212] who bears the title of the Second Adam. So, in the New Testament writings, the Second Adam is to be put using the same biblical theology of clothing. This aspect—regaining the lost glory—of the salvation narrative is echoed in the daily prayers of the Ethiopian Orthodox Church, "for through you Christ was born; the Second Adam, that he may return Adam the first man from the world into Paradise."[213]

This image of the Messiah as the Second Adam is developed in the Biblical text through one of its prominent literary forms, typology. Since the letter of the text is only a mechanism for conveying Divine revelation, the Ge'ez text

---

[209] Ibid, 87.
[210] Ibid. Regarding the garments of glory and its theological anthropology Emmanuel Gergis, *Theological Anthropology Redefined: The Theological Synthesis of Gregory of Nyssa and Ephrem the Syrian's Writings on Genesis 3:21* (Springfield: Agora University Press, 2015).
[211] Galatians 4:4-7
[212] Galatians 3:27
[213] እስመ በንቤኪ ተወልደ ክርስቶስ ዳግማይ አዳም ከመ ያግብአ ለአዳም ቀዳሚ ብእሲ እምድር ውስተ ገነት, *Wuddasay Marəyam* 6.

is here edited to fit the typological pattern and the theology of clothing-de-clothing. This may be clear for the case of the man through whom all died (Adam), and the Man by whom all have been given life (Christ the Second Adam), but where is the correlation with Joseph, who is somewhere in the middle?

The overarching typological pattern in the Biblical text is the "Son of Man," a phrase Jesus used exclusively to identify himself.[214] The title being eschatologically dense contains ideas of the ultimate destiny of humankind.[215] Embedded within the typology of the Son of Man is the Second Adam, which itself is connected to the typology of the Righteous Sufferer (e.g., Job), and this is the literary connection with Joseph—who suffered righteously.[216] Joseph in the ancient church has always been understood as a type of Christ, a shadow pointing to the Messiah.[217] Therefore, Joseph's garment was understood in the metaphysical sense, as embodiment. A Ge'ez homily attributed to Epiphanius in the *Häymanotä Abäw* speaks to this.[218]

---

[214] Leonhard Goppelt, *TYPOS: The Typological Interpretation of the Old Testament in the New*, trans. Donald H. Madvig (Eugene: Wipf and Stock, 2002), 90-107.

[215] Ibid, 90.

[216] Ibid, 100.

[217] Kristian S. Heal, "Joseph as a Type of Christ in Syriac Literature," *Brigham Young University Studies* 41.1 (2002): 29–49.

[218] This homily is located in the 57th chapter and 12th homily in the Epiphanius' tracts, see *Häymanotä Abäw*—ሃይማኖተ አበው—[*Faith of the Fathers*] (Addis Ababa, 1986), 193.

ዮሴፍᎄሞተᎄተብሎ...ይናገሩ፣ነበር፣በልብስ፣
የተረጨው፣ደም፣የርሱ፣አልነበረም፣ልብሱ፣
ግን፣የሱ፣ነበረ።እንደዚሁም፣የእስራኤል፣
ልጆች፣እጆቻቸዉን፣በመድኃኒታችን፣
በክርስቶስ፣ላይ፣ጫኑ።ወይ፣መለኮቱ፣ግን፣
መድረስ፣አልተቻላቸውም።

They said that Joseph had died, the blood which was sprinkled on his garments was not his, although the garment was his. Much like this, the children of Israel put their hands on (the body of) our Lord Christ, but they could not touch his divinity.

Therefore, the understanding of Joseph's robe by the early Church and the medieval Ethiopian Church is the metaphysical robe of embodiment. Suffering is here neither a curse nor a sign of misfortune. *Məhərka Dəngəl* was surely aiming to convey this in his introductory section in *The Chronicles of Susenyos* where he patterned *Susenyos'* misfortunes after those of God's elect. Rather, suffering is here a reality of the post-lapsarian world; after the de-clothing which is the loss of identity of the first Adam. This suffering is shared with humanity and transformed by the Messiah. For those who are clothed in Christ, the Second Adam, suffering becomes transformative and is the means by which the former glory is attained.

Conclusion

By not clinging rigidly to the text of Scripture and through an openness for obtaining better readings, some Ethiopian scholars were able to improve their Biblical text together with its commentary. From an epistemological perspective, this reveals how they viewed the linguistic characteristics of Scripture as playing a smaller part in the role of Divine revelation and how they saw the spirit of the text as sitting on a loftier plane than its language. The Ethiopian scholarship pointing to this conclusion is remembered in the oral tradition of the *Andəmta* and is directly evidenced in the text-critical mechanisms of the commentary corpus. The adage ንባብ፡ይቀትል፡ወትርጓሜ፡ ያሕዩ- "the letter kills, but the interpretation gives life"—is in fact, a hermeneutic axiom. This axiom is itself a uniquely Ethiopian commentary on 2 Corinthians 3:6.

Conclusion

The emergence of the Scriptures out of a manuscript culture has given way to the inevitability of textual variations. Ancient Jewish and Christian scribes engaged in this reality and Origen has preserved ancient variants in his Hexapla. The Hexapla evidences not only the text-critical methodology of the Early Church, but also the theological understanding of the place of language in relation to Divine revelation. It does so by preserving variant readings as objects of interpretation, to more fully understand the meaning of the passages which used these different phrases to express the Divine.

This places language below and not above the place of the text's spirit. We see here that the letter of the text is understood to function as a vehicle of Revelation, that its purpose is to reveal Him who clothed himself in our language.

The Ethiopian scholars shed light on their textual epistemology of the Scriptures through the understanding that the Lord shows through the text what His customs are in the world.[219] This phrase, taken from the heart of the Ethiopian liturgical tradition, is in its original context an explanation of how the Lord is praised in his beloved persons—quoted according to the Ethiopic Psalms and

---

[219] This quotation by *Mämǝhir* Henok is paraphrased here for simplicity. Or 'በአንድ፡አንድ፡ወዳጆቹ፡እና፡አገልጋዮቹ፡ላይ፡አድሮ፡ሥራውን፡መግለጽ፡ የተለመደ፡ነው፡ወይም፡ልማዱ፡ነው' *Mädaləw Aləbab*—መዳልወ፡አልባብ [*Treasury of Hearts*], x.

105

canticles.[220] Referencing the Psalms, this idea communicates that through His beloved persons (e.g., David, Moses, etc.), the Lord reveals His customs, and in this way He is revealed in His Personhood via relationships with humanity.

From the perspective of textual epistemology, it shows that the linguistic properties of Scripture come together to reveal the customs of God, which is the content of revelation. Given that the Scriptures are canonical texts and that their content deals with the customs of God, they provide a 'measurable' means through which humanity may encounter Him. This measurable, canonical revelation is what guides the person in their experience with the Divine Person. It is primarily in this apophatic or ineffable mystical encounter that the Ethiopian theology sees the Divine. Just as no human person can be encapsulated in notions—since as a source of life they exist dynamically and not statically— neither can God, the supreme Personal reality, and the true source of Life be confined to the notions of the Scriptural texts.[221]

This shows that the text speaks of the ontology of being as it describes the Divine Person face-to-face in dialogue and relationship to persons.[222] Unlike the Classical

---

[220] Glorified is the Lord in his holy ones [መንክር፡እግዚአብሔር፡በላዕለ፡ ቅዱሳኑ], *Ethiopic Psalms* 67:39.

[221] Dumitru Staniloae, *Orthodox Dogmatic Theology: The Experience of God, Vol. 1: Revelation and Knowledge of the Triune God*, 1st edition., vol. 1 (Brookline: Holy Cross Orthodox Press, 1998), 118.

[222] The Church Fathers speak of the dialogical role where the person (πρόσωπον), the face of God is revealed through His dialogue in the Torah, the Prophets, and the Psalms. CJ Ratzinger, "Concerning the Notion of Person in Theology.," *Communio* 17.3 (1990), 442-447.

Greek or Roman schema of person (πρόσωπον) or *persona* which are adjuncts or void pointers to being, the connection between person and being is established in the Scriptures.[223] This connection finds its nexus in the hypostatic union of the Messiah who is the culmination of the Scriptural ontology of being.[224] This hypostatic union is manifested in the robe of embodiment, communicated in the Son of Man typology. It is here that *Məhərka Dəngəl* finds the pattern of the Righteous Sufferer, where he shows how the Lord deals with persons in their suffering and how that suffering enables the recovery of not only the primordial glory, but also the eschatological—final and eternal—one that is to come.

It should be clarified that Ethiopian theology expresses '*person*' (πρόσωπον) differently than how we find it in other non-Semitic Christian theologies.[225] Regardless,

---

[223] The cosmological framework of Classical Greek or Roman philosophy did not allow for the ontological justification of being. In this framework, being is only alluded to within the imposing monism of the self-authenticating cosmos of ancient Greek thought or the Roman world's legal/organizational structure of statehood/*collegia*. In the Scriptures, the person is not an adjunct to being but is instead the hypostasis of being, the person is being itself and the most significant and constitutive element of being, see John Zizioulas, "Personhood and Being," in *Being as Communion: Studies in Personhood and the Church* (Crestwood: St. Vladimir's Seminary Press, 1985), 27–49.

[224] Additionally, the Word speaks of the Father, whose being is identified with person. God exists on account of person not on account of substance. Here, no substance or nature exists without hypostasis or person, or mode of existence. That which is the cause of existence is not substance but the person/hypostasis. Ibid, 42.

[225] This is the *akal* [አካል] which is also synonymous with *gäts* [ገጽ]. Mebratu states that both can be considered equivalent to the Greek πρόσωπον although he cautions that it does not reflect the external "observable character" as manifestation of reality. Rather it "relates to

Ethiopian theology possesses this understanding since the concept itself, even in the West, originates in and is born directly out of the spiritual data of the Scriptures.[226] The Scriptures themselves convey the concept of person in contexts and expressions that are culturally Semitic, what this means functionally is that it is expressed through an apophatic mysticism, not a systematic approach.[227]

This must be clarified to preserve the integrity of the Ethiopian perspective, which requires a refrain from the empiricism of Western theology and an avoidance of on over emphasis on scholasticism. It is also a postmark to redirect those who engage in the field, that they would steer clear of projecting the European cultural trappings onto the study of Ethiopian theology specifically or theological literature generally.[228]

Lastly, all that has been said thus far has been drawn from the masters of the biblical commentary tradition, and their perspectives and conclusions must be taken seriously by the tradition itself. If not, the Ethiopian tradition cannot progress and provide meaningful theology and answers to

the basic frame of any personal reality. Also, *akal* serves as an expression of specific essence (*baharey*) which is its origin. Thus, prosopon is not closely related to nature (*physis*), as is *akal* to *baharey*. Also, *hypostasis* may signify to some extent the same meaning as the Ethiopian *akal*, for the former is usually understood as concrete reality." Mebratu, *Miaphysite Christology*, 52.

[226] Zizioulas, "Personhood and Being," 27-35.

[227] Gergis, *Theological Anthropology*, 15. Ratzinger, "Person in Theology," 439.

[228] This issue has been seen in Syriac studies and Oriental Christian studies in general. See Gergis, *Theological Anthropology,* 16 and Brock, *The Luminous Eye,* 14.

mankind's questions. Further scholarship and effort must build upon the progress already made by the tradition. While doing so it should avoid absolutizing it or, even worse, fancifully diverging into all sorts of theological chaos and "rot of mystery." The reality is that Ethiopian theology must seriously consider the Ethiopian tradition and weigh it against the canonical revelation of God.

Bibliography

Primary Sources

Alehegne, Mersha. *The Ethiopian Commentary on the Book of Genesis.* Critical, Translation edition. Wiesbaden: Otto Harrassowitz, 2011.

August Dillmann. *Biblia Veteris Testamenti Aethiopica, in quinque tomos distributa.* Fr. Chr. Guil. Vogelii, 1853.

Bakhayla Mîkâ'êl. *The book of the mysteries of the heavens and the earth and other works of Bakhayla Mîkâ'êl (Zôsîmâs).* Translated by E. A. Wallis Budge. Berwick: Ibis Press, 2004.

Berhanu, Dawit. *Das Mashafa Mar Yeshaq von Ninive. Einleitung, Edition und Übersetzung mit Kommentar.* Hamburg: Verlag Dr. Kovac, 1997.

Beyene, Solomon Gebreyes. "The Chronicle of King Gälawdewos (1540–1559) : A Critical Edition with Annotated Translation." Staats- und Universitätsbibliothek Hamburg Carl von Ossietzky, 2016.

Cowley, Roger W. "A Ge'ez Document Reporting Controversy Concerning the Bible Commentaries of Ibn At-Taiyib." *Rassegna Di Studi Etiopici* 30 (1984): 5–13.

———. "A Geez Prologue Concerning the Work of Mämhər Kəflä *Giyorgis* on the Text and Interpretation of the Book of Ezekiel." Pages 99–114 in *Ethiopian Studies: Dedicated to Wolf Leslau on the Occasion of His Seventy-Fifth Birthday.* Wiesbaden: O. Harrassowitz, 1983.

Esteves Pereira, Francisco Maria and Sociedade de Geografia de Lisboa, eds. *Chronica de Susenyos, rei de Ethiopia.* Lisboa: Imprensa Nacional, 1892.

Getatchew, Haile ed. *THE FAITH OF THE UNCTIONISTS IN THE ETHIOPIAN CHURCH (Haymanot Mäsihawit)*. Vol. 517 of *Corpus Scriptorum Christianorum Orientalium* 91. Louvan: Peeters, n.d.

————. "THE LETTER OF ARCHBISHOPS MIKA'EL AND GÄBRƷ'EL CONCERNING THE OBSERVANCE OF SATURDAY." *Journal of Semitic Studies* 26.1 (1981): 73–78.

Kedanä Wäld, Kəflə. *Mäṣhāfä Həzqel KänäTərəgwamewu* — መጽሐፈ ሕዝቅኤል ከነትርጓሜው· *[The Book of Ezekiel with Commentary]*. Addis Ababa, 1923.

Knibb, Michael A. *The Ethiopic Text of the Book of Ezekiel: A Critical Edition*. Oxford: Oxford University Press, 2015.

Häymanotä Abäw—ሃይማኖተ አበው—*[Faith of the Fathers] (Addis Ababa, 1986 E.C.).*, n.d.

Mädaləw Aləbab YäAqwaqwam Mələkit— መዳልው: አለባብ:የአቋቋም:ምልከት *[Treasury of Hearts the Musical Notation of Aqwaqwam] (1991 E.C.).*, n.d.

Yä Gə'əz Mätshafə Qəddus—የግዕዝ መጽሐፍ· ቅዱስ. *[The Ge'ez Bible] (Addis Ababa, 2021 CE).*, n.d.

Mar Yəshäq — ማር.ይሳሐቅ *[Isaac of Nineveh] (Täsəfa Gäbərä Səlasay Press, 1982 E.C).*, n.d.

Mäṣhafä Säwasäwu Wä Mäzəgäbä Qalat Hadis— መጽሐፈ:ሰዋስው:ወግስ:ወመዝገበ:ቃላት:ሐዲስ *[Book of Grammar, Verbs, and Lexicon] (1948).*, n.d.

Wänəgel Qəddus Nəbab KänäTergwame — ወንጌል ቅዱስ ንባብ ከነትርጓሜው· *[The Gospel Text with Commentary] (Addis Ababa, 1992).*, n.d.

YäQəddus Pawlos Mäṣhäf Nəbab KänäTergwame —
*የቅዱስ ጳውሎስ መጽሐፍ ንባብ ከነትርጓሜው [The Pauline Writings
with Commentary] (Addis Ababa, 1946).*, n.d.

Secondary Sources

Allison, Dale. "Jewish Figures." Pages 11–96 in *The New Moses: A Matthean Typology*. Eugene: Wipf and Stock, 2013.

Beyene, Solomon Gebreyes. "The Tradition and Development of Ethiopic Chronicle Writing (Sixteenth-Seventeenth Centuries): Production, Source, and Purpose." Pages 145–60 in *Time and History in Africa*. Edited by Alessandro Bausi, Alberto Camplani, and Stephen Emmel. Milano: Centro Ambrosiano, 2019.

Brock, Sebastian. *The Luminous Eye: The Spiritual World Vision of Saint Ephrem the Syrian*. Revised edition. Kalamazoo: Cistercian Publications, 1992.

Budge, E. A. Wallis. *A History of Ethiopia Nubia & Abyssinia Vol.2*. Research Associates School Times Publications, 2010.

Butts, Aaron M. "Embellished with Gold: The Ethiopic Reception of Syriac Biblical Exegesis." Edited by Hans-Georg Beck. *Oriens Christianus. Hefte für die Kunde des christlichen Orients* 42.1 (1956): 409–10.

———. "Ethiopic Christianity, Syriac Contacts With." *Gorgias Encyclopedic Dictionary of the Syriac Heritage: Electronic Edition* (2020). https://gedsh.bethmardutho.org/Ethiopic-Christianity-Syriac-contacts-with.

———. "Ibn Al-Ṭayyib." *Gorgias Encyclopedic Dictionary of the Syriac Heritage: Electronic Edition* (n.d.). https://gedsh.bethmardutho.org/Ibn-al-Tayyib.

Colless, Brian Edric. "Yoḥannan of Dalyatha." *Gorgias Encyclopedic Dictionary of the Syriac Heritage: Electronic Edition* (2020). https://gedsh.bethmardutho.org/Yohannan-of-Dalyatha.

Cowley, Roger W. "A and B Verbal Stem-Type in Amharic." *Journal of Ethiopian Studies* 7.1 (1969): 1–13.

————. *Ethiopian Biblical Interpretation: A Study in Exegetical Tradition and Hermeneutics.* Cambridge [Cambridgeshire]; New York: Cambridge University Press, 1988.

————. "Mämhər Esdros and His Interpretations." Pages 41–69 in *Ethiopian Studies: Proceedings of the Sixth International Conference.* Addis Ababa: Institute of Ethiopian Studies, 1980.

————. "Preliminary Notes on the Baläandəm Commentaries." *Journal of Ethiopian Studies* 9.no 1 (1971): 9–20.

————. "The Beginnings of the Andem Commentary Tradition." *Journal of Ethiopian Studies* 10.2 (1972): 1–16.

————. "The 'Blood of Zechariah' (Mt. 23:35) in Ethiopian Exegetical Tradition." Pages 293–302 in *Studia Patristica. Vol. XVIII, 1 u Historica, Theologica, Gnostica, Biblica.* Edited by Elizabeth Livingstone. Kalamazoo: Peeters Publishers, 1989.

————. "The Standardisation of Amharic Spelling." *Journal of Ethiopian Studies* 5.2 (1967): 1–8.

————. *The Traditional Interpretation of the Apocalypse of St. John in the Ethiopian Orthodox Church.* Cambridge: Cambridge University Press, 2014.

Daniélou, Jean. *Origen*. Translated by Walter Mitchell. Eugene: Wipf and Stock, 2016.

Mebratu Kiros, Gebru. *Miaphysite Christology: An Ethiopian Perspective*. Piscataway: Gorgias Press, 2010.

Gergis, Emmanuel. *Theological Anthropology Redefined: The Theological Synthesis of Gregory of Nyssa and Ephrem the Syrian's Writings on Genesis 3:21*. Springfield: Agora University Press, 2015.

Goppelt, Leonhard. *TYPOS: The Typological Interpretation of the Old Testament in the New*. Translated by Donald H. Madvig. Eugene: Wipf and Stock, 2002.

Getatchew, Haile. *A Catalogue of Ethiopian Manuscripts Microfilmed for the Ethiopian Manuscript Microfilm Library, Addis Ababa, and for the Hill Monastic Manuscript Library, Collegeville, Vol. VI: Project Numbers 2001-2500*. Collegeville: Hill Monastic Manuscript Library, 1982. http://archive.org/details/EMMLCatalog06.

———. "Highlighting Traditional Ethiopian Literature." *Silence Is Not Golden: A Critical Anthology of Ethiopian Literature*. Lawrenceville: Red Sea Press, 1995.

———. "Review of Ethiopian Biblical Interpretation: A Study in Exegetical Tradition and Hermeneutics." *Journal of the Royal Asiatic Society of Great Britain and Ireland* 2 (1990): 378–82.

———. "Review of The Traditional Interpretation of the Apocalypse of St John in the Ethiopian Orthodox Church (University of Cambridge Oriental Publications, No. 33)." *Rassegna Di Studi Etiopici* 30 (1984): 186–91.

Hassen, Mohammed. "Review of Futuh Al-Habaša: The Conquest of Abyssinia [16th Century]." *International Journal of Ethiopian Studies* 1.2 (2004): 177–93.

Heal, Kristian S. "Identifying the Syriac Vorlage of the Ethiopic History of Joseph." Pages 205–10 in *Malphono W-Rabo d-Malphone Studies in Honor of Sebastian P. Brock*. Piscataway: Gorgias Press, 2008.

————. "Joseph as a Type of Christ in Syriac Literature." *Brigham Young University Studies* 41.1 (2002): 29–49.

Henze, Paul B. *Layers of Time: A History of Ethiopia*. London: C. Hurst & Co, 2000.

Kee, Howard Clark, Eric M. Meyers, John Rogerson, Amy-Jill Levine, and Anthony J. Saldarini. *The Cambridge Companion to the Bible*, 2007.

Knibb, Michael A. "Review of The Traditional Interpretation of the Apocalypse of St. John in the Ethiopian Orthodox Church." *Bulletin of the School of Oriental and African Studies, University of London* 48.1 (1985): 146–47.

Knibb, Michael Anthony. *Translating the Bible: The Ethiopic Version of the Old Testament*. LOCALE; British Academy, 1999.

Lee, Ralph. *Symbolic Interpretations in Ethiopic and Ephremic Literature*. Vol. 24 of *Eastern Christian Studies*. Leuven: Peeters, 2017.

————. "The Ethiopic 'Andəmta' Commentary on Ethiopic Enoch 2 (1 Enoch 6–9) - Ralph Lee, 2014." *Journal for the Study of the Pseudepigrapha* 23.3 (2019).

Littmann, Enno. "Abyssinian Apocalypses." *The American Journal of Semitic Languages and Literatures* 19.2 (1903): 83–95.

Malan, Solomon Caesar. *The Book of Adam and Eve, Also Called the Conflict of Adam and Eve with Satan, a Book of the Early Eastern Church, Translated from the Ethiopic, with Notes from the Kufale, Talmud, Midrashim, and Other Eastern Works,* London: Williams and Norgate, 1882.

Martin, Matthew J. "Origen's Theory of Language and the First Two Columns of the Hexapla." *The Harvard Theological Review* 97.1 (2004): 99–106.

Metzger, Bruce M. *The Early Versions of the New Testament: Their Origin, Transmission, and Limitations.* Oxford: Oxford University Press, 1977.

Michelson, David A. "Philoxenos of Mabbug." *Gorgias Encyclopedic Dictionary of the Syriac Heritage: Electronic Edition* (2020). https://gedsh.bethmardutho.org/Philoxenos-of-Mabbug.

Miles, John Russiano. *Retroversion and Text Criticism: The Predictability of Syntax in an Ancient Translation from Greek to Ethiopic.* Chico: Society of Biblical Literature, 1985.

Moreschini, Claudio, and Enrico Norelli. *Early Christian Greek and Latin literature: a literary history.* Translated by Matthew O'Connel. Peabody: Hendrickson Publishers, 2005.

Nazianzus, St Gregory of. *On God and Christ: The Five Theological Orations and Two Letters to Cledonius.* Crestwood: St. Vladimir Seminary Press, 2002.

Nersessian, V. "Roger Cowley (1940-1988)." *Journal of Ethiopian Studies* 22 (1989): 171–77.

Orlinsky, Harry M. "The Columnar Order of the Hexapla." *The Jewish Quarterly Review* 27.2 (1936): 137–49.

"Ostrich | Habitat, Food, & Facts." *Encyclopedia Britannica,* 5 July 2020. https://www.britannica.com/animal/ostrich.

Pankhurst, Richard Keir Pethick. *A Social History of Ethiopia: The Northern and Central Highlands from Early Medieval Times to the Rise of Emperor Tewodros II.* Trenton: Red Sea Press, 1992.

Pedersen, Kirsten. "The Amharic Andemta Commentary On The Abraham Stories Genesis 11:24-25:14." *The Book of Genesis in Jewish and Oriental Christian Interpretation A Collection of Essays.* Edited by J. Frishman and L. Van Rompay. Traditio Exegetica Graeca. Louvain: Peeters Publishers, 1997.

———. *Traditional Ethiopian Exegesis of the Book of Psalms.* Wiesbaden: Otto Harrassowitz Verlag, 1995.

Ratzinger, CJ. "Concerning the Notion of Person in Theology." *Communio* 17.3 (1990): 439–54.

Salvesen, Alison G. "Syro-Hexapla." *Gorgias Encyclopedic Dictionary of the Syriac Heritage: Electronic Edition* (2020). https://gedsh.bethmardutho.org/Syro-Hexapla.

Staniloae, Dumitru. *Orthodox Dogmatic Theology: The Experience of God, Vol. 1: Revelation and Knowledge of the Triune God.* Vol. 1. Brookline: Holy Cross Orthodox Press, 1998.

Stoffregen- Pedersen, Dr. Kirsten. "The Ecumenical Theological Research Fraternity in Israel," 21 November 2019. http://www.etrfi.org/stoffregen--pedersen-dr-kirsten.html.

"Strong's Greek: 243. Ἄλλος (Allos) --Other, Another," 14 July 2020. https://biblehub.com/greek/243.htm.

"Strong's Greek: 1125. Γράφω (Graphó) -- to Write," n.d. https://biblehub.com/greek/1125.htm.

"Strong's Greek: 2087. Ἕτερος (Heteros) -- Other," 14 July 2020. https://biblehub.com/str/greek/2087.htm.

Taddesse Tamrat. *Church and State in Ethiopia, 1270-1527.* Oxford: Clarendon Press, 1972.

Thomas Oden, and Curt Niccum, eds. *The Songs of Africa: The Ethiopian Canticles.* New Haven: ICCS Press, 2017.

Wechsler, M. G. *Evangelium Iohannis Aethiopicum Aeth. 109.* Louvain: Peeters Publishers, 2005. Wright, Jessica, Leon Grek, and Leonardo Cohen. *The Jesuits in Ethiopia (1609-1641): Latin Letters in Translation.* 1st ed. Edited by Wendy Laura Belcher. Wiesbaden: Harrassowitz Verlag, 2017. https://www.jstor.org/stable/j.ctvckq54b.

What Is the Bible?: The Patristic Doctrine of Scripture. Edited by Matthew Baker and Mark Mourachian. Minneapolis: Augsburg Fortress Publishers, 2016. https://www.jstor.org/stable/j.ctt17mcsbk.

Zizioulas, John. "Personhood and Being." Pages 27–49 in *Being as Communion: Studies in Personhood and the Church.* Crestwood: St. Vladimir Seminary Press, 1985.

About the Author

Alem Sahle holds Bachelor of Science degrees in Physics and Computer Science from the University of Maryland and a Master of Theological Studies from Agora University. He works as an aerospace engineer with a focus on embedded spacecraft flight software, particularly supporting earth science related instruments already in flight. He also serves as a deacon in the Ethiopian Orthodox Diocese in Washington DC. His research interests are mainly focused on Biblical studies, the Ethiopian commentary tradition, and the liturgies of the Ge'ez rite.

Printed in Great Britain
by Amazon

46241068R00067